Music and Singing Early Years

Music and singing are an inherent part of children's lives and offer a wonderful opportunity to promote young children's learning and development. This how-to guide is full of useful information to support musical understanding and assist practitioners in developing their knowledge, skills and confidence in planning and leading successful and enjoyable musical activities in a range of early years settings.

Focusing on the role of singing and children's musical learning at various stages of development, *Music and Singing in the Early Years* aims to demystify music by providing practical tips, ideas and information on the integration of musical activities in the early years curriculum and environment, and provides clear explanations of musical concepts.

Chapters consider topics such as:

♩ vocal strategies and development

♩ using song, rhyme and movement

♩ integrating instrumental accompaniments

♩ observation and assessment

♩ planning and delivery

♩ resources for music making.

This book is essential reading for all early years practitioners looking to improve their musical understanding and plan successful musical activities with young children.

Zoe Greenhalgh is well known for her work as an Early Childhood Music educator, writer, researcher and consultant. In addition to providing bespoke workshops for Early Years and Music practitioners, she has written accredited programmes for organisations such as the British Kodály Academy and Edge Hill University, UK, where she is an Associate Tutor in Early Years Education. Zoe is a course mentor for the groundbreaking Certificate for Music Educators: Early Childhood at the Centre for Research in Early Childhood in Birmingham, UK.

Music and Singing in the Early Years

A Guide to Singing with Young Children

Zoe Greenhalgh

Routledge
Taylor & Francis Group

LONDON AND NEW YORK

First published 2018
by Routledge
2 Park Square, Milton Park, Abingdon, Oxon OX14 4RN

and by Routledge
711 Third Avenue, New York, NY 10017

Routledge is an imprint of the Taylor & Francis Group, an informa business

British Library Cataloguing in Publication Data
A catalogue record for this book is available from the British Library

Library of Congress Cataloging in Publication Data
A catalog record for this book has been requested

ISBN: 978-1-138-23321-8 (hbk)
ISBN: 978-1-138-23323-2 (pbk)
ISBN: 978-1-315-31001-5 (ebk)

Typeset in Optima
by Out of House Publishing

Contents

Acknowledgements   vii

Introduction   1

1 **Musical development**   5

2 **Melodic matters: singing games and rhymes**   17

3 **Rhythmic roots**   33

4 **Developing a song**   43

5 **Planning and evaluation**   53

6 **Putting the planning into practice**   69

7 **Resources for music making**   79

   Glossary   97
   Sources of further information   101
   Index   103

Acknowledgements

I have learned a great deal from some truly inspirational women over the years: Helga Dietrich, Lucinda Geoghegan, Dr Alison Street and Dr Susan Young. I would like to thank them for their support and generosity in sharing their wealth of knowledge and expertise over the years. My heartfelt gratitude is also extended to my sister-in-law Chris Fitt for giving me her undivided attention in editing and proofreading the manuscript of this book. The dedication however has to be to my late mother who filled my childhood with singing and music and was forever reminding me about my book writing idea and urging me to 'hurry up and get on with it'!

Introduction

Singing is an important way of interacting musically with young children. In early childhood, singing songs is a way to develop, enrich and consolidate a wide range of knowledge and skills, both musical and non-musical (Chen-Hafteck and Mang 2012).

> *The smaller the children the more important singing is for them. They like it!*
>
> (Blandford and Knowles 2016, p. 291)

Therefore the ability and confidence to sing is an important skill for an early childhood teacher (Swaine and Bodkin-Allen 2014; Gray and MacBlain 2015).

For children singing is a natural and enjoyable everyday activity. Their adult carers and educators are often not so sure, with many believing that they themselves are unmusical. Music education has been a low status area for decades, resulting in a widespread lack of musical knowledge, confidence and skill among much of the adult population.

The most effective practitioners are those who have a passion for what they do, who continually work to develop their skills and knowledge, and who constantly strive to be the best that they can be. We all have our own particular areas of expertise which combine to make a rich and varied environment. Mine is singing with young children, yours may be language development or model making. We are all on a continuum of learning within our many fields of knowledge and have a greater level of expertise in some areas than in others. Whether we are at novice level or somewhere in the middle, however, is not so important. What *is* really important is that we acknowledge where we are and seek to improve, to up our game and move in the right direction to develop our knowledge and skill further, as described by the Japanese concept of Kaizen – the practice of continuous improvement. When new knowledge for the science curriculum is required, we research and learn. It is the same with music and singing, only this research and learning requires practical skills rather than using a book or website.

The thought of singing is outside the comfort zone of many practitioners, and the idea of singing solo completely terrifying! I am sorry, but I cannot teach you to sing through the pages of a book; like most things in life, the only way to improve is to practise. Help is at hand though, in the form of digital apps (for your mobile phone, tablet or computer) which can help you to learn to sing better, with the added bonus that they can be used in the privacy of your boudoir or garden shed!

It has to be said, though, that there is no substitute for singing with others. There are many community choirs and choirs for 'non-singers' each with their own genre of music (including pop, rock, gospel, musical theatre) which usually welcome new members. You never know, you may really enjoy it, make new friends and discover your hidden Pavarotti or Adele! Why not start a regular staff singing session in a lunch hour? Not only will this singing with others improve your own singing, it will also be enjoyable and may benefit your personal health and well-being. You can also develop your singing along with the children – what a fantastic experience for them to support their 'teacher's' learning as you support theirs!

There are countless music resources available to early childhood practitioners,[1] but these do not provide the confidence, knowledge and skills required to use them effectively. I have visions of song books, bought with great enthusiasm, gathering dust on shelves in store cupboards, and it is this that has provoked me to write this book – a handbook to singing with young children, containing information and practical ideas for practitioners to dip into and support them in their work. Given the vast number that are widely available, I have chosen not to include any songs and rhymes in this book. I have, however, provided some recommendations of where suitable resources might be found.

My intention is to support practitioners to develop their singing skills and musical practice: to provide basic musical 'nuts and bolts' information and give practical tips and ideas about why, what and how to lead young children in singing and related musical activities. This 'how to…' guide for the teacher contains clear, practical information including:

♩ the knowledge and preparation necessary for success

♩ choosing appropriate songs to sing

♩ use of props

♩ playing instruments

♩ working within a physical space

♩ organisation of children and additional adults

♩ creating a positive, nurturing approach

♩ next steps…

In short, I wish to help to demystify music and make singing with young children more enjoyable!

Note

1 The term 'leader' is used throughout this book and refers to anyone who sings with young children, e.g. Teacher, Early Years Practitioner, Music Educator, Librarian, etc.

References

Blandford, S. and Knowles, C. 2016. *Developing Professional Practice 0–7.* 2nd ed. Abingdon: Routledge.

Chen-Hafteck, L. and Mang, E. 2012. Music and language in early childhood development and learning. In McPherson, G. E. and Welch, G., eds. *The*

Oxford Handbook of Music Education. Oxford: Oxford University Press, pp. 261–74.

Gray, C. and MacBlain, S. 2015. *Learning Theories in Childhood*. 2nd ed. Los Angeles: SAGE.

Swaine, N. and Bodkin-Allen, S. 2014. Can't sing? Won't sing? Aotearoa/New Zealand 'tone deaf' early childhood music teachers' musical beliefs. *British Journal of Music Education* 31(3), pp. 245–63.

Musical development

From the start I would like to dispel the myths that only a few are musically talented and that only some of us can sing. The fact of the matter is that

We are all musical; we just need the opportunity.

(Welch 2017)

From the very earliest days of life babies have a highly developed sense of hearing with a finely tuned sense of pitch. By the twenty-sixth week of pregnancy hearing is fully developed and babies are listening, interpreting and learning from the voices and sounds that surround them.

There is evidence that parents, siblings and others in all countries and cultures are subconsciously 'programmed' to use Infant Directed Speech (IDS), also known as motherese, when interacting with infants (Young, V. 2017). At a higher than normal pitch, this 'sing-song' style of speech involves the use of short phrases with exaggerated, lengthened and repeated words often combined with exaggerated facial expressions and movement. Babies find this form of speech highly attractive and they respond by attempting to reproduce the variety of melodic sounds they hear, sounds that are characteristic of their 'mother tongue', and that play an important role in language learning and musical development. Every language has its individual soundscape which the use of motherese exaggerates. The intonation and contours of the mother tongue are further exaggerated through

Infant Directed *Singing*, also referred to as 'singese' (Young, V. 2017; the term was coined by Dionyssiou), which combines words, melody and emotion to create a unique and powerful form of communication that is even more alluring to the young child (Trehub 2003a).

Although most infants do not learn to talk until their second year, their voices are there for us to hear from birth.

(Selleck 1995)

Learning to sing is very much like learning to speak. If from the start of life a baby is immersed in an environment full of speech, she wants to join in and makes every effort to do so, producing increasingly skilful attempts to imitate what she hears. This practice is rewarded by positive, uncritical responses from her carers which encourage her to keep trying and learn more. It is exactly the same with learning to sing. What makes a 'musical' child is not some innate genetic ability or talent, but a positive and supportive home environment where music and singing are part of the fabric of everyday life. Musical children tend to inhabit musical homes or attend musically rich playgroups, nurseries or schools.

A baby's first toy is her voice, with which she experiments, honing her skills and gradually gaining control. Early 'cooing' develops into short musical babbling phrases at around 2 months of age, which by 3 to 4 months have become short snippets of melody imitating the shape of the voices and language she hears (Williams 2013). By 4–5 months, her vocal musical play shows clear links with the intonation and characteristics of the language she hears most from her home environment, her 'mother tongue', which plays a significant role in her musical and singing development. The baby can only copy and learn from her own experience and so the more 'musical' the speech and singing she hears in her local environment, the more she will try to imitate and learn (Williams 2013).

What gives us the capacity to think is the quality of a baby's exchanges with other people over the first eighteen months of life.

(Hobson 2002)

Infant Directed Singing (Trehub 2003b) is even more attractive to the very young, making singing games and rhymes with young children a powerful and influential activity. Songs and rhymes provide examples for the baby to copy, encouraging her to play with sounds and learn how to communicate with others effectively. This musical exchange is a continuous, active and dynamic process requiring total engagement of all participants. The 'game' develops, increasing her anticipation of the final 'punchline'. Each contribution is offered in relation to the previous one, in an accumulative, cyclical process which builds up shared understanding between the players (Young, S. 2005). Both parties are then rewarded: the baby by the positive attention she receives and the play-partner by the success of the baby's contributions. Gopnik et al. (1991) describe this as 'pillow talk' as it is rooted in mutual love and affection, and Malloch (2002), who has written extensively on early interaction with babies, calls it

> Communicative musicality...the dynamic sympathetic state of a human person that allows coordinated companionship to arise.
> (Malloch cited in Trevarthen 2002, p. 21)

In her work with Baby Room practitioners, Vanessa Young (2017) has identified a 'spectrum of vocal utterances' as a broad definition of what is involved in musical communication with the very young, expanding the meaning of 'song' in this context.

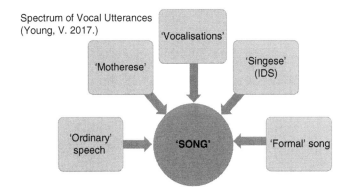

Young also writes about the ways in which singing and song can promote Connections, Closeness, Confidence and Communication – the '4 Cs' – with parents and caregivers (Young, V. 2017, p. 259). Self-image begins at birth in direct response to the reactions (words and body language) of those around them. Quality time spent singing with a child, particularly by a significant carer, therefore enhances attachment and builds emotional security.

Every time you smile and interact warmly with a baby, you help to sow seeds of a positive image.

(Tassoni 2001)

It is generally recognised that personal success in life is dependent on positive self-esteem. Individuals with high self-esteem are generally more successful in forming stable relationships, coping with new situations and achieving their academic potential.

Learning musical skills

Right from the start, life is inherently musical. From the earliest spark of life (i.e. before birth) until she can walk independently, a baby experiences steady beat (pulse) through the motion and movement of daily activities: for example, regular footsteps when being carried, being rocked, patted, stroked, bounced and so on. Once the child walks unaided, this physical experience of steady beat is reduced and this learning may be lost unless it is supported in some other way. So why does this matter?

A continuous pulse provides the foundation upon which all music sits; consequently the ability to *feel* a steady beat within oneself is a fundamental musical skill. Children often find this less straightforward to achieve than reproducing the rhythm of a song (which is usually defined by the words).

The role of singing

Musical activity, particularly singing, demands focused attention and careful listening – important skills for all areas of learning. Singing games and rhymes involve listening, timing and turn-taking – all fundamental elements for successful conversation – and provide a place to practise, gain experience and unconsciously learn these vital skills in a playful and social manner. Songs and rhymes develop sequencing ability, as they have a natural form and structure with a beginning, middle and end.

Young children's vocabulary is enhanced and expanded through playful exploration of songs and rhymes; children will happily sing words that are not in their spoken vocabulary and children with speech disorders such as a stammer are empowered by the ability to respond naturally, without impediment, and interact on an equal footing with their peers.

Through musical activity children play, develop their communication and social skills, and express their feelings. Music, and singing in particular, affects our mood, and in early life they play an important role in emotional regulation. For example, lullabies, one of the oldest and culturally universal forms of children's song, are sung to calm and soothe the young child and ultimately induce sleep. In contrast, play songs are used to divert children's attention and maintain good humour, for example when waiting for a bus or doctor's appointment, or during long journeys.

Vocal development

In the earliest days of life a baby uses her voice to attract attention from caregivers and to communicate feelings such as hunger and distress. At birth, the structure of the larynx (voice box) is different from that of an adult and it develops significantly over the following eight years (Williams 2013). In the first few years of life this means that the child has a limited vocal range in terms of pitch and is unable to sing loudly.

All of us are capable of singing, although, like most things in life, accurate singing takes a great deal of experience and practice. In the earliest days the infant is influenced by the speech and singing that she hears in her local environment and this develops as the child matures, so that at:

o 2 months she is babbling musically in relation to the contours of the mother tongue;

o 3–4 months she can imitate the exaggerated contours of her mother tongue;

o 4–5 months she plays with and explores the voice musically;

o 1–2 years she is able to spontaneously sing a short phrase many times at higher and lower pitches;

o 2–3 years her singing is linked with activity, frequently when at play. Examples might include: chanting, spontaneous 'free-flow' singing with no sense of structure, combining sections of known songs often referred to as pot-pourri songs (Moog 1976), and sounds relating to animals, machines or physical movement.

Susan Young (2003, p. 87) suggests that 3-year-old children are the most prolific spontaneous singers in nursery settings. Older pre-schoolers are inclined to talk more and sing less and as the educational environment becomes more formal, spontaneous singing becomes less common, going 'underground' to less structured places, such as the playground and the home.

Learning to sing

Children's singing development has been identified as having four phases (Welch 2006, p. 317):

1. At the start, it is the words that are the centre of interest with children making 'chant like' vocalisations limited to two or three pitches.

2. This is followed by a growing awareness that changing vocal pitch is a consciously controlled process, a skill that can be mastered. With

practice and experimentation, the child's singing becomes gradually more accurate, using an expanding range of pitches.

3. Control of the voice develops, with the ability to sing *sections* of the song accurately, but not necessarily the entire song. Sometimes lines from different songs are 'sewn' together to form a 'potpourri' song (Moog 1976).

4. Finally, the ability to sing simple songs with pitch and rhythmic accuracy develops.

Why sing with young children?

Music has an infinite capacity to affect brain and body. It can act as a unifying force and a vehicle by which other skills can be developed, enjoyed & understood. As such, music can be a powerful means of learning.

(Goddard Blythe 2004)

Firstly, and most importantly, I would say that singing is worthwhile for the sheer pleasure of it, as an everyday activity to be enjoyed, particularly when shared with others. Our voice is a central part of our personal being and an integral aspect of our identity. Using our voice to sing is therefore an expression of self and has profound links with our physical, social, emotional and intellectual well-being. Singing can also be a shared, flexible and interactive activity and should always be positive and enjoyable.

But it can be so much more than this, particularly in early childhood.

♩ Social interaction is enhanced through singing, especially on an intimate, one to one basis, and from the earliest days helps to create a closeness between participants and builds emotional security. Even very young babies will respond to songs and rhymes that are often repeated if given time and encouragement to do so. Quality one to one interaction makes the child feel valued and builds emotional security, thus providing a firm basis for future learning and development.

♩ To sing is to express your individuality. Singing activities offer young children an opportunity to be imaginative and express themselves without fear, to choose an action, animal or subject in a safe and nurturing environment where all contributions are valued. When such contributions are valued by others, the child's self-confidence is enhanced, helping to establish a positive self-image.

♩ Singing in a group develops social skills – the children learn to cooperate with others, to share, listen, take turns, etc.

♩ Singing games and rhymes demand active participation from all involved. By their very nature they offer an alternative mode of engagement which impacts positively on children's concentration and group cohesion. Consequently, children who have learning or behavioural difficulties frequently find singing and music a pleasurable experience, often enabling them to enjoy the rare satisfaction of success and achieve positive recognition from their peers, parents and teachers.

♩ Singing purely for pleasure or maybe laughs! Children learn best when they are enjoying themselves and rhymes and songs are often full of humour and delight.

♩ Traditional folk and children's songs are rooted in cultural heritage, enriching the children's understanding of their place in the world.

Singing for musical reasons

♩ *Everyone* has a voice. It is an instrument that is a) free, b) portable and c) by far the most direct and natural way of making a musical sound. No external manipulation or coordination is required in contrast to playing a violin or recorder, for example.

♩ When singing, the music is experienced physically through bodily action as well as being heard as sound: truly multi-sensory learning. Consequently, anything learned through singing is mastered more deeply and thoroughly.

♩ In early childhood children need to be immersed in music and singing in the same way that they need to be immersed in a language-rich environment. Through singing, children gain unconscious understanding of musical concepts without the need for labels, notation or theoretical knowledge. The technical language and musical literacy can be explored at a later stage.

♩ Singing develops musical memory: the words combine with the melody to give the song shape and structure and provide memorable features. Though imitation, learning and repetition of songs and rhymes a song bank is built to share with family and friends.

♩ Singing is vital for developing inner hearing: the ability to 'hear' how the music sounds inside your head, in the same way that we read without speaking. This is essential for true musical understanding.

♩ Singing 'live', rather than singing along to recorded music, is immensely valuable. Recorded music is passive, one-dimensional and prescriptive with no flexibility or sense of interaction between performer and listener. It is thought that babies are unable to process the multiple layers of sound that many commercially produced recordings contain (Young, V. 2017).

♩ The ability to pitch the voice accurately is learned through singing solo. When we sing with a piano or recorded backing track we 'lean' on the pitch provided. When singing along to the radio we can – to our ears – sound fantastic, but we may not actually sound quite so accomplished when it comes to singing the same song unaccompanied!

And finally, singing is every child's birthright…

A totally natural and inclusive activity that is free and available to all.
Anytime, anyplace, anywhere.
No equipment required.
The human voice – Everybody has one!

References

Goddard Blythe, S. 2004. *The Well Balanced Child*. Stroud: Hawthorne Press.

Gopnik, A., Meltzoff, A. and Kuhl, P. 1991. *How Babies Think*. London: Phoenix.

Hobson, P. 2002. *The Cradle of Thought: Exploring the Origins of Thinking*. London: Macmillan.

Moog, H. 1976. *The Musical Experience of the Pre-School Child*. London: Schott.

Selleck, R. 1995. *Managing to Change*. E Cowley: National Children's Bureau.

Street, A. 2018. Playful meaning making in music with young children and parents. In Goodliff, G. et al., eds. *Young Children's Play and Creativity: Multiple Voices*. Abingdon: Routledge, pp. 127–39.

Tassoni, P. 2001. Self-esteem: I'm OK! *Nursery World*. [Online] 16 October Available from: www.nurseryworld.co.uk/nursery-world/news/1085215/self-esteem-im-ok [Accessed 21 July 2017].

Trehub, S. 2003a. Toward a developmental psychology of music. In Avanzini, G. et al., eds. *The Neurosciences and Music*. Annals of the New York Academy of Sciences 999. Boston: Blackwell, pp. 402–13.

Trehub, S. 2003b. Musical predispositions in infancy: an update. In Peretz, I. and Zatorre, R., eds. *The Cognitive Neuroscience of Music*. Oxford: Oxford University Press, pp. 3–20.

Trevarthen, C. 2002. Origins of musical identity: evidence from infancy for musical social awareness. In MacDonald, R., Hargreaves, D. J., and Miell, D., eds. *Musical Identities*. Oxford: Oxford University Press.

Welch, G. 2006. Singing and vocal development. In McPherson, G., ed. *The Child as Musician*. Oxford: Oxford University Press, pp. 311–29.

Welch, G. 2017. Keynote speech. EuNet MERYC Conference, Homerton College, Cambridge.

Williams, J. 2013. *Teaching Singing to Children and Young Adults*. Oxford: Compton Publishing.

Young, S. 2003. *Music with the Under-Fours*. London: RoutledgeFalmer.

Young, S. 2005. Musical communication between adults and young children. In Miell, D., MacDonald, R. and Hargreaves, D. J., eds. *Musical Communication*. New York: Oxford University Press, pp. 281–301.

Young, S. 2009. *Music 3–5*. London: RoutledgeFalmer.

Young, V. 2017. You sing, I sing, we both sing, we all sing. In Goodliff, G. et al., eds. *Young Children's Play and Creativity: Multiple Voices*. Abingdon: Routledge, pp. 257–65.

Melodic matters
Singing games and rhymes

2

Young children like to sing and vocalise when they play, and they learn best when they are enjoying themselves. As children are sociable beings who enjoy playful interaction with their peers, singing games offer an excellent way for them to learn without even realising what is occurring!

In early music education, it is not necessary or important that the children know which concept or skill they are learning or doing. Knowing the *name* of these skills does not bestow the ability to perform them, as music cannot be produced through words, only through action. The correct vocabulary will of course eventually be necessary, but not until each skill has been honed through weeks or months of repeated practice in a variety of ways with different activities. This approach is highly positive and makes failure all but impossible; the children learn unconsciously through play and their ability is only openly assessed when the skill has already been mastered. What *is* vitally important is that the children enjoy what they are doing, that they are engaged and that they interact in playful activities with their peers in a positive and nurturing environment.

Babies and young children find a singing voice much more attractive than a speaking voice, so singing is a valuable way to communicate and engage their attention. 'Teacher talk' is not always necessary and is often overused, leading to the children losing focus and switching off. The young learn naturally through imitation, copying the actions and vocalisations of those around them. As the leader, just singing and doing (modelling) in a playful and positive manner is therefore a highly effective way to elicit children's participation and focus, while maintaining the playfulness and enjoyment of the activity. As the leader, however, it is very important to:

a) choose an appropriate song/rhyme in order to achieve your aim,

b) know precisely what you want the children to do to achieve this aim, and

c) make sure that you provide a clear and accurate model for the children to copy.

Using movement and/or a game with songs and rhymes adds to their power, making the value of the whole activity greater than the sum of its parts and embedding learning though multi-modal means. Repetition is also very important, as children like to revisit familiar songs, rhymes and stories. Repeating these activities a number of times, both within the session and over subsequent days/weeks, builds confidence, encourages participation and consolidates skills.

Once a song or rhyme becomes very familiar it is then possible to develop the 'game' by adding layers of complexity to deepen learning and enhance enjoyment, such as incorporating creative movements, introducing instrument playing or adjusting the activity to meet fresh objectives. In this way learning is scaffolded, multimodal, social and fun.

Over time, through experience and thorough knowledge of these well-chosen songs, the child gains an understanding of how pitches are sequenced (melodic building blocks) and how sequences can be combined to create music: i.e. an aural understanding of 'musical grammar' – harmonic form and structure – with which to play, improvise and compose. This whole process is akin to the unconscious, but supported, way in which children's speech and language skills develop – sounds combine to form words, then words are sequenced to form sentences. This internalised understanding of the sounds of music or language then forms a strong basis for future exploration and development.

Games and rhymes provide scope for a wide range of child-friendly approaches through which musical learning can be achieved, such as:

♩ children moving or dancing, individually or as a group, performing simple movements, e.g. copying the teacher, choosing their own actions or acting out the words. Straightforward, and requires the least skill on the part of the child

♩ partner games (children working in pairs, adult+child or child+teddy), e.g. clapping games, dancing pairs, rowing boats, 'knee bob' activities, interactive sharing, tickling rhymes, finger plays

♩ team working, e.g. 'wafting' Lycra/parachute, line and circle games

♩ games with a solo role, such as walking/chasing around a circle or singing alone. This requires more confidence

♩ use of puppets and other props

♩ pretend play and make-believe, generating imaginative ideas and responses.

Learning in such a playful and child-friendly manner develops musicianship.

♩ Children become familiar with the sounds, form and structure of music and – with no need for reading or writing – begin to understand how they might fit together. *Sound* therefore comes before *sight*.

♩ Starting with simple activities and songs, then building up the complexity gradually in small, but logical, steps enables the child to succeed. Success breeds confidence and increases the desire to learn more.

♩ Over time, unconscious knowledge is labelled so that the children learn both the appropriate vocabulary to describe their experience, and then the symbol which represents it (i.e. notation). In this way, musical literacy can be taught in a practical, logical and achievable sequence.

Supporting children's musical learning

As an early years educator, it is important to have an understanding of suitable approaches, resources, musical progression and next steps. Songs and music are used in many areas of learning, not just for music education per se. The song, however, should always be well chosen and the performance musically secure. This is particularly important in early childhood, where musical learning comes from experience and is 'caught' rather than 'taught', emphasising the impact of good modelling and the need for practitioners to develop the associated knowledge and skills.

Also of great importance is the need for children to be exposed to an eclectic range of musical styles, genres and modes of participation. There is, after all, an aesthetic aspect to music that needs to be conveyed if the child is to enjoy an enriched lifespan of musical engagement, as identified in Article 31 of The United Nations Convention on the Rights of the Child:

> *1. States Parties recognize the right of the child to rest and leisure, to engage in play and recreational activities appropriate to the age of the child and to participate freely in cultural life and the arts.*
>
> *2. States Parties shall respect and promote the right of the child to participate fully in cultural and artistic life and shall encourage the provision of appropriate and equal opportunities for cultural, artistic, recreational and leisure activity.*
>
> (UNICEF UK 1989)

Well-known traditional songs are also of great value. These songs have been sung for many years – some for centuries – and form an important part of cultural heritage. As such, even if they feature language that is no longer in common usage, they remain important works of art which still have a place in the twenty-first century.

> *A wonderful song does not wear out, but delights over and over again. Nor does it go out of fashion [...] It is the imagery of the poem that makes a song art, not its objective accuracy. A song in which a*

child can imagine [...] herself as a bluebird or as a 'bell-horse' is of greater artistic value than one in which [...] she is 'a good little child who always looks both ways when crossing the street.' Just as in great poetry, images in songs of nature or of the past are more likely to transport the child beyond his concrete, everyday existence into the realm of ideas and dreams where art rules.

(Forrai 1998, p. 16)

Voice and ear training

To reproduce a song accurately a child needs to have heard it often enough to acquire an internalised picture of its form and shape. To sing it in tune, the ability to control the physiology of the vocal chords is also necessary. The development of singing skills, therefore, requires constant repetition and many years' practice starting from the time they find their singing voice, usually somewhere between 2 and 3 years of age. Some children appear to naturally sing in tune, some don't, but with practice and encouragement all will sing well, with very few exceptions.

In humans, the singing voice is naturally higher in pitch than the speaking voice. Children's voices, both speaking and singing, are generally higher in pitch than adults'. For young children, the natural range at which the child's vocal 'equipment' is able to sing is generally from the D above middle C upwards to B (a range of a major 6th) (Williams 2013). So, the most accessible songs for young children to sing successfully fall completely within this pitch range, from the first to the last note. Men's voices are of course generally lower, and children take this for granted; therefore, as a rule, men do not need to alter the pitch of their voice to sing with young children.

Learning to sing

Rhythmically simple songs and rhymes, often containing recurring words and phrases, are taught by listening and repetition. Some adults might find songs of this nature limited and tedious, but children like singing them and find them easier to commit to memory. The leader sings the song providing a good model for the children to reproduce. This ties in with Bandura's social learning theory of the important role of modelling by adults and other children within the group, with much early learning deriving from the child observing and actively imitating their actions (David et al. 2003). With this in mind, to provide good role models think about how you can make use of additional adults, or children with more developed skills.

Singing requires two fundamental skills: the ability to reproduce a heard pitch accurately (pitch matching) and being able to sing a pitch precisely in relation to those that precede and follow it (relative pitch). This results in the ability to 'sing in tune'. In early childhood, voice play is of great value as it gives the child knowledge of their own vocal range and capabilities, e.g. exploring the voice through 'sirening' and animal or machine sounds.

♩ Use voice play to accompany stories or to illustrate movements throughout the day, e.g. a descending vocal slide, '*weeeee*', as a child or book character comes down a slide, or making animal sounds when playing or telling a story.

Solo singing

Singing solo with no accompaniment of any kind helps to secure voice control and develop pitch matching skills, so it is important to offer many opportunities for solo responses right from the start. The opportunities become more formal as confidence and skill develops.

♩ Sing a short phrase for a child to echo, one which requires an identical response of words and melody, e.g. repeating a sung phrase, such as '*Hello Bobby*' to Bobby the puppet. It is often useful to ask another adult to go first, to model the response, or to choose a *confident* child – be aware that if the first one 'bottles out', the rest probably will too!

♩ Use a pop-up puppet; if the child sings solo, the puppet rewards the child by popping up and showing itself. A magic box or book can also be used for the same purpose; the child taps the box/book with a magic wand while singing a song. The solo singing could be the song itself or the 'magic word' at the end. The book/box 'decides' on the reward depending on the child's performance.

♩ Giving the child a puppet or toy and asking it to sing, rather than the child, is often a successful ploy to encourage a less confident child to participate, as the attention of those watching is then transferred from the child to the puppet.

♩ Progress to a sung call & response format such as:

   ○ the leader singing, 'Hello Oliver'; child replying, 'Hello Zoe'; then

   ○ expand on this by improvising simple question & answer phrases of similar length, e.g. 'What would you like to eat?' 'Apple and banana'.

♩ Introduce circle games which require a child to sing a solo.

♩ Sing individual phrases of a well-known song, e.g. two finger puppets singing lines in turn to each other. This activity can also be used in a group situation with children taking turns to sing each line (shows phrasing and helps develop inner hearing).

♩ Use songs that start with a child singing a solo line for the rest of the group to copy. This is particularly useful to support a child who has difficulty matching the pitch of the rest of the group; the rest of the group will copy the lead child's starting pitch ensuring that this individual will know what it *feels* like to sing in tune with others.

♩ If after much practice some children are still not able to pitch match, sing the phrase again without comment but at a slightly slower tempo to give the child the chance to hear more clearly. Be careful not to imply any judgement so that the child does not lose confidence. Maybe use a puppet or make a game of it.

In addition to children who sing with their speaking voice (sometimes dubbed 'growlers'), some children may sing much too high and need to learn how to sing lower. Either way, to help those who struggle to find their singing voice:

- ♩ use voice play to explore the range of their voice. Try animal sounds immediately followed by a song, e.g. before singing a song about a cat, ask the children to say 'miaow' – a sound which is instinctively produced at a higher pitch – which will raise their singing voice to a more appropriate pitch for the song.

- ♩ position a 'struggling' singer next to a child who is a strong singer to provide support.

Remember!
The child's response is *never* wrong, merely 'different' or a variation. For some children it may take quite some time to learn pitch control as this requires *lots* of experience.

Developing inner hearing

In order to develop children's inner hearing (i.e. an internalised sense of pitch, having a good 'ear') it is important to use songs that the children already know well. This familiarity means that the child has a complete knowledge of all aspects of the song and can sing it without thinking.

- ♩ Use a pop-up puppet as the 'conductor' to control the dynamic (volume) of the singing:
   - ○ puppet up = sing using a louder voice
   - ○ puppet down but still visible = sing using a quieter voice

And when this is well established,

   - ○ puppet disappears = no sound. The children are now using their 'thinking voice' (i.e. inner hearing). Ask the children *What happened? Where did the voice go?*

It is helpful for the puppet to sway gently to the steady beat throughout the song as a visual prompt (i.e. showing the steady beat). This is particularly important when the thinking voice is used. Let the children take turns to control the puppet and lead the group. This is more complex than it might at first appear!

♩ Using a well-known song children sing lines in turn; the song is complete but none of the children are singing all of the time. Knowing the song well means that children can sing their phrases confidently and without hesitation when it is their turn to sing. This also emphasises the phrasing and structure of the song.

♩ Use a thinking voice for some song phrases or sections so that these sections are not audible and the child has to 'hear' them internally in order to sing the next phrase.

Remember!
Continue all actions/movements throughout the whole song/rhyme to show continuation of the music during silent beats.

Relative concepts

This refers to musical concepts such as **pitch** (higher/lower), **tempo** (faster/slower) and **dynamics** (louder/quieter).

Pitch – higher/lower

For this concept, higher and lower are more accurate terms to use than high and low as the pitch of one note can only be described in relation to another. For example, with two *different* notes that could be described as low, one of them must be a lower pitch than the other.

This relative concept is difficult for young children to grasp as it is very abstract. It therefore requires much supported experience.

♩ Make the pitch 'visible' by using movement (hands, body, Lycra or parachute) to follow the pitch contour of a song, e.g. a higher note = arms in the air, and a lower note = arms down. In addition, when using rhymes, the pitch of the spoken voice can be changed as suggested by the words: raised for words such as 'up' or 'high', lowered for 'down' or 'low'.

♩ 'Playing' the song on the body using actions that spatially represent the tune. For example, sing a simple four-beat phrase such as 'Hel-lo Fred-dy' using the pitches of the 'cuckoo' call twice – higher, lower, higher, lower. This is an interval of a minor 3rd interval or s-m in Solfa.

- o touch shoulders (both hands) for the higher pitch

- o touch thighs for lower pitch

- o i.e. shoulders, thighs, shoulders, thighs

♩ Guessing game – the leader's two finger puppets sing, one higher pitch, one lower pitch. *Which one sang higher?* Encourage the children to listen carefully by not using the physical position of the puppets to show which is which.

Tempo – faster/slower

It is important that children experience this concept and learn to 'play' with tempo. Think about ways to extend this into other activities, such as reading stories aloud. For example, in Alice in Wonderland the character of the White Rabbit is most appropriately portrayed using a quick and energetic style of voice.

Dynamics – louder/quieter

Similar principles to those detailed above also apply to the development of this concept. However, be aware that using a vertical physical movement to visualise dynamics is not recommended as it will conflict with those used to teach the concept of pitch.

Remember!

To develop these concepts successfully it is important that the children know the songs/rhymes well to begin with.

Finding a voice and learning to sing

Singing with babies

Musical development begins pre-birth, so educating mothers, family and carers to sing with their baby from the start is very important.

As discussed previously, all babies have a very well-tuned 'ear' and can hear the slightest change in pitch. They are also very musical with their voices, cooing and gurgling in tune with the songs they hear. When singing or talking in the expressive way we naturally do with babies (Infant Directed Speech or motherese) our voices are of great interest to them, impacting on their emotional state and sense of security in addition to conveying words and tunes.

♩ Songs and rhymes with young babies are best shared on a one to one basis (preferably parent/carer and child) with lots of eye contact and mirroring of vocalisations and movement. Touch is also very important.

♩ Songs and rhymes have equal value. At this stage, not all songs need to be limited in pitch and range as the baby will not yet have 'found' her singing voice. Some *simple* songs should be included, however, as the baby will be constantly playing with her voice and attempting to reproduce what she hears. Perfection is not a necessity! However, from the music education angle, singing should ideally be as accurate as possible so that the baby has a good role model to copy.

♩ Using clear rhythmic movements, touch the baby or move her body to the steady beat/rhythm of the song. Remember, the steady beat continues through any silent beats which may occur in the middle or at the end of the song.

♩ The game or emotion of the song/rhyme is all-important. Songs and rhymes need to be taken at a slow pace, clearly and expressively performed using *big* facial expressions and loving physical contact. Give the baby time to respond (up to 10 seconds), and then react to her response. Repeat this cycle many times until the baby knows it well enough to anticipate what comes next (tickle, fall, etc.).

♩ Insert the baby's name into the song/rhyme to make it more personal.

♩ Once familiar with the activity, play with the song/rhyme, e.g. vary the tempo, pause in the middle, build up to the punchline. Give time for the baby to fill in the gaps. This is important for learning the rules of conversation.

♩ Pick up clues; read the signs. Does the baby want more? Has she had enough? Is a new game required or does she need to calm down?

♩ Above all:

COMMUNICATE   **INTERACT**   **PLAY**

Toddlers: finding a singing voice

Children generally begin to sing in a more sustained fashion between the ages of 2 and 3 years. The *main* musical aims with this age group are a) to encourage confident, accurate singing, both in a group and solo, and b) to develop the child's sense of steady beat.

♩ Encourage voice play to give the children experience of the full capabilities of their voices and help them to gain control (slides, sirens, etc.). Use different voice timbres, i.e. different 'voices': speaking, singing, whispering, higher, lower, spikey, robot (monotone), giant, fairy, growly, posh, tired, smiley and so on. Use these different voice timbres when telling stories and saying rhymes and encourage the children to use them as well.

♩ Choose simple repertoire; lots of repetition within songs/rhymes is useful. Sing them slowly enough for the syllables to be heard clearly and reproduced accurately. Repeat many times without stopping, to give the child time to become familiar with it and pluck up the courage to join in.

♩ **LISTEN** to the children singing. Assess what you hear and, if necessary, adjust the tempo accordingly.

♩ Offer the children many different opportunities to sing, especially solo, both planned and spontaneous. Be aware that some children do not respond well to being 'put on the spot' and may offer their contribution at a different time such as when it is another child's turn to sing. In situations such as this, be careful to value *all* contributions whenever they occur – as long as they can do it, the *when* is not important. If treated sensitively, children's confidence will grow.

♩ Encourage solo singing using the echo and call & response techniques discussed earlier. If the child does not respond, it should not be treated as an issue. Some children take time to build up sufficient confidence and/or listening experience to do this. Smile and be inclusive and perhaps offer the child an alternative way to respond. How about a wave? The child will then feel able to join in with the singing when they are ready to do so.

♩ Give children the opportunity to choose an action, partner, colour, etc. This helps to increase their self-confidence and offers a sense of ownership.

♩ When children lack confidence, give them the choice to do the activity with a friend, adult or prop of their choice, instead of on their own, to bolster confidence. **Never force participation**; some children need to spend time watching and listening before they are ready to join in.

3 to 5 years

♩ Include more songs than rhymes, gradually increasing the range and complexity as the children's capabilities progress.

♩ Use echo and question & answer songs, as mentioned earlier. These are good for practising pitch matching, turn-taking and listening and help to develop knowledge of musical form and structure.

♩ As the children's confidence and skills grow, more challenging games, which may incorporate more complex individual roles, can be introduced.

♩ Develop musical 'ear' and voice control by encouraging children to match your pitch (unconsciously at first).

♩ For example:

  o children echo a given phrase such as: *'Goodbye Evie'* (leader) *'Goodbye Zoe'* (child's response). At first, use the same tune for every child (e.g. the two-pitch 'cuckoo' call), then

  o expand the number of pitches, varying the combinations used. This will create greater musical understanding and give the child a repertoire of melodic building blocks with which to play and improvise.

  o The child may improvise a response rather than giving an exact echo, either of which is fine. Ask if the child's response was 'the same or something different'. Turn this into a group activity by introducing hand movements to denote 'same' and 'different'. In this way, all children can be involved and you can assess individual children's progress.

♩ Using songs the children know well, include activities to develop inner hearing, relative pitch and an understanding of musical form and structure.

Above all, encourage children to vocalise and play with their voices and ensure that singing is always a positive affair, a joyful mode of communication and self-expression.

References

David, T. et al. 2003. *Birth to Three Matters: A Review of Literature.* Nottingham: DfES Publications. [Online] Available from: http://webarchive. nationalarchives.gov.uk/20130404090533/https://www.education.gov.uk/ publications/eOrderingDownload/RR444.pdf [Accessed 20 July 2017].

Forrai, K. 1998. *Music in Pre-School*. Brisbane: Clayfield School of Music.

UNICEF UK. 1989. *The United Nations Convention on the Rights of the Child*. [Online] Available from: www.unicef.org.uk/what-we-do/un-convention-child-rights/ [Accessed 17 July 2017].

Williams, J. 2013. *Teaching Singing to Children and Young Adults*. Oxford: Compton Publishing.

3 | Rhythmic roots

To support children's rhythmic development the use of movement with all activities is essential. This is not 'movement to music', however, but movement as an accompaniment to the singing. Using simple actions, acting out the words, and simple dance steps or gestures emphasise the rhythmic qualities of the song. The older the child, the more complex the movements can be.

> All rhythmic training in the kindergarten must be in the context of songs and rhymes, i.e. living music. Having children march in a circle to a drum beat or while clapping is an unmusical exercise. It only serves to drill attention and discipline and does not promote the child's development as an active independent individual.
>
> (Forrai 1998, p. 54)

Rhythmic development

The stages of rhythmic development are:

1. Establishing a strong sense of steady beat

2. Recognising and reproducing rhythmic content of songs

3. Combining steady beat and rhythm.

Steady beat (pulse)

This is the heartbeat of the music.

➢ *Features:* Regular and unchanging. Continues though 'silent' beats right to the end of the song or rhyme.

➢ *Identifying a steady beat:* Soldiers march to the steady beat of the music. We walk and climb stairs to a steady beat.

Steady beat provides the foundation of all music, the structure upon which it is built. To make sense of music the ability to feel a steady beat is therefore a fundamental and essential skill.

From the very earliest days of life babies have a wealth of steady beat experience: pre-birth they hear their mother's heartbeat and the 'whooshing' of the placenta; as an infant they are rocked, patted, carried (feeling the motion of the adult's footsteps) and bounced, all movements that are conducted to a steady beat. Once they are walking and moving around independently this everyday steady beat reinforcement is lost.

No matter how old the individual, a sense of steady beat has to be felt internally before it can be reproduced accurately. In my experience, children generally find tapping the rhythm of songs straightforward, probably because the words create the rhythm, making it easier to identify. Keeping the steady beat (through movement or instrument playing) while singing (rhythm) requires the words and the steady beat to fit together, a skill that needs to be experienced and practised before it can be internalised.

So, *before* it can be securely internalised a steady beat needs to be:

o experienced, e.g. through knee riding games ('knee bobs')

o felt in the upper body, e.g. clapping, tapping

o felt in the lower body, e.g. stamping, stepping

Developing a sense of steady beat

The continuity of the steady beat is reinforced by movement, i.e. kinaesthetic learning in which learning is through bodily action. In every song and rhyme movement of some form is a must. With all children and adults performing even the most simple of actions, the whole group is actively involved and feels the satisfaction of being a synchronised part of the group. These movements will also support the learning objective (such as showing a steady beat or rhythm, awareness of form or structure).

Sometimes the actual learning is not in the most conspicuous place. For example, in a circle game with an individual part, where the attention is on one child moving around the rest of the group, the speed (tempo) of the song may be slower than the child's comfortable walking pace. The rest of the circle however will move together, tapping the steady beat on their legs as modelled by the leader. It is this leg tapping that provides the focused learning experience of keeping a steady beat and is reinforced through repetition as many children take their turn to walk around the circle.

Actions performed to a steady beat, such as leg tapping, walking, clapping, etc., provide a natural opportunity to assess the child's stage of learning through observation within the session.

Remember!

The steady beat movements must continue through any rests (i.e. gaps, silences).

Some actions are harder to perform than others, e.g. walking the beat is harder than clapping or tapping. A child may be able to keep a steady beat but might not *yet* have sufficient motor skills to perform the action modelled.

Ideas for practising steady beat

1. Speaking and tapping

Speaking and tapping in time provides another vehicle for feeling the steady beat and can be used as an enjoyable game in many contexts throughout the day.

The shortest phrase that makes musical sense is four beats long, so a four-beat question & answer activity (*with associated movements*) is really useful. Simple to incorporate into daily activities it could, for example, be used when taking the register:

Teacher				Emily Holt			
♥	♥	♥	♥	♥	♥	♥	♥
Good	**Morn**-ing	**Em**-i-ly	**Holt**	**Good**	**Morn**-ing	**Miss**-is	**Smith**

Another idea is to use a call & response format. For example, after a story or song about buying something at the shops the leader might ask a child what was bought. The leader models first, then children copy without dropping a beat:

Leader				Group repeats			
♥	♥	♥	♥	♥	♥	♥	♥
What did	**Ol**-i-ver	**buy?**	(silent)	**What** did	**Ol**-i-ver	**buy?**	(silent)

Leader or child				Group repeats			
♥	♥	♥	♥	♥	♥	♥	♥
Ol-i-ver	**bought**	**saus**-a-	**ges**	**Ol**-i-ver	**bought**	**saus**-a-	**ges**

Be aware that:

➢ although the fourth beat may be a rest (i.e. silent), the steady beat is still there and needs to be represented by an action: e.g. the one used for the rest of the phrase, or perhaps by another action to show that it is a silent beat and therefore different from the others;

➢ some words and names have the stress on the second syllable, e.g. Jo-**an**-na or po-**ta**-to. If this occurs at the start of the phrase, the first syllable will come *before* the first beat (known as an anacrusis or up-beat).

♥	♥	♥	♥	
Jo-	**an**-na	**bought**	**saus**-a-	**ges**

Physically showing the steady beat (e.g. tapping legs) as well as saying the words is important. Do not alter the normal pattern of speech to fit to the steady beat, thereby ensuring that the natural stresses and patterns of the language remain unchanged.

2. Singing in time to a regular action

Ideas for use with:

♩ infants: rocking, carrying, patting, bouncing, etc.

♩ toddlers/preschool: digging, hammering, walking upstairs, swinging, clapping, jumping, rocking on a see-saw, etc.

3. Saying a rhyme to a steady beat, for example:

♩ a 'dipping' rhyme (e.g. 'One potato, two potato...') to choose a child for an activity – point to or tap each child in turn to the steady beat and ask the children to join in. The child pointed to on the last beat of the rhyme is chosen.

♩ to give the children a time limit to carry out an instruction. For example, by the end of the rhyme the group should be sitting down in a particular place or the children should have found partners.

4. In other areas of learning

For example, reciting number sequences, tables, rhymes or lists of *any* kind. Using a steady beat with some associated simple movement will aid memory and help the children to keep together, providing them with a predictable structure within which they can respond. As humans, we find working together in this way very satisfying.

Rhythm

➤ *Features:* Irregular and changing, and may include silent spaces (rests). Often there is more than one note per beat.

➤ *Identifying rhythm:* In the songs and rhymes used in early childhood the syllables in the text usually correspond to the rhythm, i.e. one syllable per note.

As with all new learning, much unconscious experience and physical practice are required to develop the child's skills and understanding of rhythm.

At this early stage of musical learning, songs or rhymes comprising very simple note lengths are the most appropriate, as follows:

Symbol	Duration	Traditional name	Solfa name
♩	1 beat	crotchet	ta
♪	½ beat ♫♫ or ♫ = ♩	quaver	te
𝄽	1 silent beat	crotchet rest	sh

Ideas for practising rhythm

♩ 'Make your hands say the words.' While singing aloud, use actions or movements to the *rhythm* of the song or rhyme as opposed to the steady beat. Make sure the song/rhyme you choose has a varied rhythmic pattern, such as ♩♫♩♫ or ♩♫♫♩, so that the rhythm is clearly different from the steady beat and can be easily identified.

♩ The shortest phrase that makes musical sense consists of four steady beats. Using this as a framework, clap or tap a rhythmic pattern for the children to copy, such as:

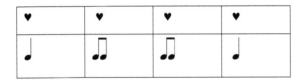

o 1st four beats – leader claps rhythmic phrase

o 2nd four beats – children echo

o 3rd four beats – leader claps the same or a new rhythm

o 4th four beats – children echo

This can be used between the leader and child, child and group *or* child and child. Make sure that the continuity of the music (i.e. the steady beat) is maintained throughout.

This technique can be used throughout the day either as a playful 'filler' in the transitional times between activities or as a method of gaining the children's attention.

♩ Same or different? Can the children identify whether you are tapping the steady beat or is it 'something different'?

♩ Representing duration with movement. Use a movement to represent a specific note length. For example, where the rhythm ♫ occurs, tap shoulders twice and for ♩ clap hands once. Each tap/clap represents a note within the song, a sort of movement notation which can be incorporated quite simply into traditional style clapping games.

Rest

➤ *Feature:* A silence or gap in the music. This may occur in the middle or at the end of the song or rhyme. The steady beat continues through the rest, resulting in a silent beat, whereas in the rhythm it will create an empty space.

Ideas for practising rests

♩ In an activity in which the children are performing an action to the steady beat (e.g. tapping, clapping, stepping, playing an instrument, etc.) this action will continue throughout the whole song, occurring in the rests in the same way as it does in the other beats. Initially it is vital that the child experiences the steady beat as continuous and unchanging throughout the entire song/rhyme. Depending on the nature of the action used, this may mean that the rest is not actually silent, but as all beats are marked in an identical way, every beat becomes equal.

♩ The main feature of a rest is that it is silent. It is not, however, empty, as the song continues through the rest. Making the rest 'visible' within an activity allows the children to understand that it exists but, as it has no sound within the music, it is appropriate that this representation is also without sound.

Once a sense of steady beat has been consolidated, rests can be emphasised by using a different action. For example:

♩ the rest provides a space within which an action happens, such as pretending to toss a pancake, throwing a bean bag, jumping over something or turning to a new partner.

♩ a song with rests that the children know well is sung by the group with its associated actions. The children take it in turns to demonstrate an action of their choice to represent the rest and model it for the rest of the group to copy. This offers the opportunity for great personal expression and creativity, and often much hilarity as funny facial expressions or strange physical movements are used. Discussion about which choices were most 'fit for purpose' can then follow, thus connecting musical features (theory) with the movements chosen and the acquisition of appropriate language; for example, did the movement interrupt the continuity of the steady beat/rhythmic flow and therefore alter the music as a whole?

Form and structure

Like poetry, all songs and music have an identifiable structure. Many of the simple songs and rhymes sung with young children consist of four lines with four beats in each. Individual lines are often repeated – words, melody and rhyme – or maybe the melody and rhythm repeat with different words. For example,

Rain, rain, go a - way,

come a - gain a - noth-er day.

Lit - tle John-ny wants to play,

rain, rain, go a - way.

When written in this way it is clear to see that lines 1 and 4 are identical in all aspects, and lines 2 and 3 have the same rhythm and melody, i.e. the same musical content, but different words. Understanding the structure of songs and rhymes is highly valuable as this enables us as music educators to use movements or a game to demonstrate the structural features. In this song, for example, use one action for the identical lines 1 and 4 to emphasise the rhythm, and an alternative action for the identical lines 2 and 3, thus visibly demonstrating that the rhythm of these lines is *not the same* as that of lines 1 and 4. In this way the children gain knowledge of form and structure through playful and unconscious means.

Reference

Forrai, K. 1998. *Music in Pre-School*. Brisbane: Clayfield School of Music.

Developing a song

I have written several times within this book about developing a song in order to extend children's learning, knowledge and understanding of music. This section is intended to illustrate how this song development might work in practice and provide you with some ideas.

When introducing a new song it is important to present it in a manner that both attracts the children's attention and enables accurate memorising of the tune, rhythm and words. The way the song is modelled at this early stage is particularly important, as this is the version that the children will remember; it is much easier to learn correctly in the first place than it is to correct inaccuracies at a later date! The leader, therefore, needs to know the song thoroughly and be able to sing it from memory at an appropriate tempo, while clearly demonstrating the movements/actions for the children to replicate. As a rule, new material will need to be introduced at a tempo that enables the children to clearly hear the details of the words and tune, but not so slowly or pedantically that the overall musicality of the piece is lost.

As always, some form of movement or a game are essential elements of all musical activity. These actions are usually vital to the learning objective so, particularly with a new song/rhyme, they will need to be easy to perform in order to enable the children to 'catch' the song and participate successfully without being distracted by over-complicated and challenging actions.

Here are a few ideas on how one particular song can be developed. These activities are not connected exclusively to this song but are used here to spark you into thinking of ways to develop the songs and rhymes *you* use with the children *you* work with.

Swing me over the water

Unaccompanied singing with movement

♩ 'Row' a boat. Sing the song several times with pairs of children (or one child + one adult) sitting cross-legged on the floor, face to face, holding each other's hands while rocking backwards and for-wards in time to a steady beat. As always, sing the song *at least* twice without stopping – however many continuous repetitions you decide on, be consistent so that the children know the 'rules of the game' from the outset.

This activity can then be:

o used as a purposeful 'filler' to occupy short spaces of time, e.g. before lunch

o repeated at transitional times in the day as a gathering or group cohesion activity, such as when waiting for children to hang up their coats. Those waiting patiently on the carpet will enjoy singing a familiar song with their friends, and the children you are waiting for will hear the singing and are likely to move a bit more quickly to ensure they do not miss out!

o slotted into stories in which related activities occur, e.g. a boat ride, a swing or tea time

o used in the wider environment to accompany similar-themed activities, such as playing on a swing, with water, with small world figures or with teddies in the home corner.

Using Lycra

Gather a group of children around a piece of Lycra (approximately 1.5 metres square). Holding the edge of the fabric the group works together, moving the material to the steady beat while singing the song.

The tune of this particular song lends itself to the fabric being raised and lowered according to the shape of the melody – *up* when singing the higher note, *down* when singing the lower note – thus making the pitch structure of the song visible. With a different song it might be more appropriate to move the fabric in an alternative fashion, such as from side to side/backwards and forwards.

This whole group movement is a particularly valuable way to support children's experience of a steady beat as it is very difficult in these circumstances for any individual to move at a different time or in a different direction to the rest. Manipulating *where* children sit within the circle enables certain children's learning to be enhanced. Placing a child with less developed skills between two more accomplished peers, for example, will reinforce that child's experience of steady beat by synchronising the movements of all three.

Because of the elastic properties of Lycra it is possible for the children to all row in and out at the same time, stretching and releasing the tension on the fabric as they move. This requires more consolidated skills than before as each child has to control his own actions, moving independently but synchronised with the rest of the group.

Put a teddy on the top of the fabric to be rocked throughout the song and then tossed into the air at the end. All children move together to ensure the best jump possible with a 'one…two… three…WHEEEEEEEE!'. To make the teddy leap high into the air requires self-control and teamwork – good listening, cooperation and awareness.

Using a companion song/rhyme

Alternate this song with another appropriate song or rhyme, e.g. Song x 2, Rhyme x 1, and repeat as required. This intermittent rhyme could be specially written for this particular purpose or could be an existing rhyme. If the main song is new to the children, it is good to use a familiar companion song/rhyme. For example:

When singing *Swing me over the water* using Lycra with a teddy on top, as above, one option might be to use the traditional rhyme

Fishes in the water, fishes in the sea,
We all jump up with a one...two...three!

...while moving the fabric briskly from side to side, to a faster steady beat than that used for the song. On the words *'one'* and *'two'* move the Lycra up and down more deliberately in preparation for a mighty joint effort to propel the teddy skywards on *'three'*.

At first the children are usually very excited by a teddy on the Lycra and are desperate to make him jump. Repeating the familiar rhyme *Fishes in the water* a few times, with its jumps for Teddy at the end, provides a way to progress to moving on to the song – in this instance, *Swing me over the water* – in which Teddy is rocked more gently to 'give him a rest after all that jumping'. This development in the activity prompts the children to exercise some self-control and participate, confident in the knowledge that Teddy will jump again in the rhyme once the song has been sung the requisite number of times.

Tip: Using a song/rhyme which is already familiar is very helpful in certain situations. When working with a new group of children and/or parents, for example, starting with something that the group already knows builds confidence and encourages participation. As a result, building positive relationships with participants (adults as well as children) becomes easier to achieve.

♪ The children are rowing boats in pairs singing the main song. A shorter companion song/rhyme is introduced during which the children get up, find a new partner and sit down ready to row and sing the main song again. This entire sequence must be completed within the length of time it takes to sing the companion rhyme so that the two songs/rhymes join together seamlessly.

Using songs in the ways described above:

♪ facilitates many repetitions of the song, providing unconscious experience of the identified musical aim, building musical memory and consolidating learning

♪ develops team working, listening and awareness. For example, the children need to work together, waiting until the moment comes when they can make Teddy jump high and straight. This requires that every individual child listens, watches and is fully engaged in the here and now, i.e. demonstrating 'sustained attention, goal-directed behaviour, and cognitive flexibility' (Hallam 2016), all activities which are associated with executive functioning of the brain and self-regulation

♪ requires the children to use their memory to anticipate how much time there is before the end of the song/rhyme and organise themselves to complete the required actions within this time frame.

Other ways to present the song

♪ Singing the song in a different style, such as a lullaby, could be a useful way to wind down after a more exuberant activity, or to enact a scene from a story. Singing it as a lullaby turns the musical performance into a quieter, more gentle style of singing which requires different awareness and skills, facilitating conversations around voice timbre, expression, dynamics, tempo and so on. This activity broadens children's repertoire of musical expression, to be reused, explored and extended at will during free play or continuous provision.

♩ Organise older children into 'boats' with a 'passenger' on board: two children stand facing each other, arms outstretched at shoulder height, holding their partner's hands. A third child stands in the space between their arms, i.e. 'in' the boat, facing one of the other children, resting their hands on those of their friends. While the song is sung the boat sways gently to the steady beat, from side to side. On the silent beat (rest) at the end of the song, the side of the boat 'opens' (arms higher up in the air on the relevant side), so that the passenger can leave the boat and move to another. And then the whole process begins again!

Once the children are familiar with the song there are any number of extension ideas depending on the particular group of children. For example:

♩ Introduce a rhyme or chant between repetitions of the song (companion rhyme) to restrict the time available to move to another 'boat' – take too long and the child is left to sink in the briny sea!

♩ Add to the excitement and drama of the activity by adding or removing extra players (e.g. the leader) to alter the number of berths available for the passengers!

This requirement to work in partnership with others and maintain focus enables children's musical skills to be enhanced by:

♩ consolidating learning through movement to a steady beat

♩ developing their musical memory, their knowledge of form and structure, and the anticipation of what comes next. This internalisation of the song enables the children to a) 'open' the boat at the appropriate moment, i.e. in the rest (silent beat) at the end of the song, and b) know exactly how much time they have to find a new boat

♩ offering further opportunities to practise their singing and pitch matching. In addition, as the boat personnel change the children will have to listen *to*, and sing *with*, a variety of different voices of varying quality and timbre.

Adding an instrumental accompaniment

The timbre and texture of songs and rhymes can be altered by extending the activities to include the playing of *tuned* or *untuned* instruments. Simple untuned percussion instruments – wood blocks, maracas (shakers), guiros, drums, etc. – are common features in early childhood. These are instruments which the children can use expressively and creatively, gaining much musical knowledge and skill in the process. It is also important however that children experience tuned instruments – chime bars, bells, xylophones, etc. Nicola Burke (2017) likens instruments to pencil crayons. Untuned instruments are equivalent to monochrome lead pencils which children are more than happy to use in many highly creative and satisfying ways. Tuned instruments, on the other hand, like colour pencils, add a whole new realm of possibilities to this monochrome world, thus expanding the creative process through the introduction of pitch.

The addition of instrumental accompaniment to songs and rhymes that the children have been working on, and know very well, extends musical and learning experience. This can start very simply and gain in complexity as the children's skill develops.

Remember!

Using only one or two instruments to accompany the song will ensure that the singing voices are not overwhelmed and that the musicality of the activity is not lost. It will also provide the opportunity/excuse to repeat the song many times to give a number of children the opportunity to play the accompaniment. Children should always be encouraged to continue to sing even if they are playing an instrument.

Here are a few suggestions of how instruments might be used:

Incorporate one or two untuned instruments to change the timbre of the song and add to the soundscape; in this song ('Swing me over the water'), a child could play a wave drum to provide the sound of the sea.

A harmonic accompaniment could be played on tuned instruments such as chime bars. If the purpose of the activity is to show a steady beat or the rhythm, it may be helpful for the child to play one instrument with the leader/adult playing a second, thus providing a model for the child to copy.

In terms of which chime bars to play, it is most useful in this case to use the highest and lowest pitches of the song, which are the first and last notes. This provides an interval of a perfect 5th: A and the D below (*s* and *d* in relative Solfa), an interval which will work well with most pentatonic children's songs.

The addition of this simple harmony changes the sound, enabling the children to hear the notes they are singing *in relationship to* the accompaniment. This encourages the development of more refined listening skills and promotes the awareness of relative pitch – i.e. the relationship between one pitch and another – a fundamental requirement for singing 'in tune'. Once again it is important to remember that young children may find it challenging to hear pitch accurately from anything other than a human voice. Consequently, *simple* sung harmony would be a more helpful way for children to learn to pitch accurately and to sing in tune. However, at this early stage young children are generally not able to sing in two parts successfully without a great deal of prior experience. With a song the children know extremely well and sing confidently, a possible alternative might be for an adult to sing the harmony part, blending in with the children's voices without overpowering them.

With a more experienced group it may be possible to extend the instrumental accompaniment, gradually adding further complexity and variety. For example:

♩ Initially both pitches are played together (i.e. the highest and lowest pitches of the song, as above), progressing to playing alternate beats beginning with the lower pitch (D) so that the pitch *sung* and the pitch *played* on the instruments are different throughout the song with the exception of the final note.

♩ The children play an ostinato (short repeated rhythmic pattern) on untuned instruments as an accompaniment. This is a short rhythmic sequence that is seamlessly repeated, over and over, as an accompaniment throughout a piece of music. This sequence usually, but not always, mirrors a rhythm that occurs within the song.

This chapter is intended to illustrate a few of the infinite ways in which songs and rhymes can be presented and developed in order to facilitate musical learning. However, it is not the activities per se that are important but the underlying purpose and design, namely a child-friendly, playful, and positive approach, intelligently crafted as a powerful and effective way to progress children's music education.

References

Burke, N. 2017. Research on the benefits of music and movement. *Early Years Summit*, Autumn 2017. [Online] Available from: http://live.earlyyearssummit.com/ [Accessed 28 October 2017].

Hallam, S. 2016. The impact of actively making music on the intellectual, social and personal development of children and young people: a summary. *Voices: A World Forum for Music Therapy*. Special Issue, 'How Music Can Change Your Life and the World' Vol 16, No 2. [Online] Available from: https://voices.no/index.php/voices/article/view/884/725 [Accessed 24 August 2017].

5 | Planning and evaluation

Planning, both long and short term, is a vital element in supporting and advancing children's music knowledge and skills, and is a process that begins with careful consideration of the areas of learning to be covered by each group of children. To be truly effective, these learning objectives should be considered and clearly expressed using SMART criteria: Specific, Measurable, Achievable, Realistic and Timely.

Identifying objectives in the short term and over time is important from a preparation perspective, as this gives clarity to the design of the curriculum ensuring that all aspects of musical learning are included in an appropriate and cohesive manner. This not only clarifies the progression of children's learning but also, most importantly, acts as the framework for the necessary assessment, reflection and evaluation of the programme in terms of the:

a) children's learning and progression

b) content and concepts covered

c) approaches to teaching and learning used

d) leader's/additional adult's personal professional development

e) available resources.

Assessment against these objectives will identify improvements or adjustments that can be made to inform future planning and provision, thus ensuring the programme is 'fit for purpose' and that children's learning progresses well.

Learning objectives and content therefore need to be considered

a) long term, i.e. yearly and beyond

b) medium term, i.e. termly

c) short term, i.e. individual sessions and weekly planning

before selecting your material and resources.

Consider the following factors as you devise your plans:

♩ People – who will be involved?

- o The children. To devise an effective curriculum it is important to know the group – every group is different in terms of age, stage of development, prior knowledge, specific needs, group dynamics, how well you know them, size of group, etc. This may mean that some elements of planning can only be identified *after* you have met the group.

- o The adults. Who are they and what is their level of knowledge/ confidence/experience? A group with parents will require a different approach to one without. The number of adults attending (e.g. early years practitioners) and the child:adult ratio are also important factors to consider.

- o Expectations. As practitioners we often have to conform to the expectations of parents, employers, managers or funders in addition to national Early Years educational guidelines and statutory requirements.

♩ Aims and objectives:

- o Music learning – keep your identified *main* musical aims in mind and design the plan accordingly (e.g. moving to a steady beat, singing at pitch, etc.).

- o Holistic learning – social and emotional development, communication and language, interaction, concentration, etc.

♩ Physical environment:

- The nature of the physical space available – the size of the room, any hazards or distractions, acoustics, ambient noise, etc. We may have no control over many of these factors and so need to plan with them in mind, identifying teaching strategies which maximise the potential for children to learn in a positive and constructive environment.

♩ Time (temporal) considerations:

- Number of weeks/sessions available

- Length of sessions

- Repetition of content by others beyond music sessions. If planned sessions only happen once a week it is important that some element of repetition of the activities occurs, preferably on a daily basis in between, thereby reinforcing the learning. For young children one half-hour session in a week with no subsequent repetition is probably little more than entertainment – a week is a long time in a small child's life! Ideally the regular practitioner/teacher, parent or carer needs to not only be present but also participate in the activities so that this repetition can occur throughout the week. If you lead music sessions either as a visiting music specialist or with a group of children you do not work with on a daily basis, this has to be considered in the planning process. This will also require you to provide resources such as song sheets and/or activity plans/explanations.

- Time of day and context, e.g. how the session fits within the setting's day. It is also helpful to know what activities precede and follow the session.

- Time of year – seasons, festivals, etc. in terms of session topics and possible periods of reduced attendance.

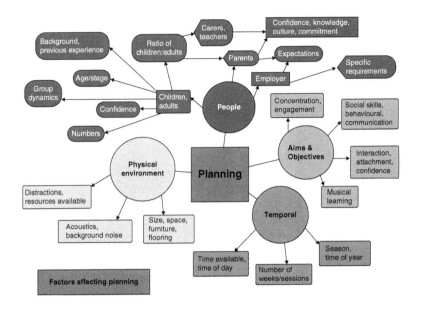

Remember!

Look after your voice!

> **Please consider** the acoustic environment within which you work and how this might impact on your voice.

> **Do not** strain your vocal folds by trying to compete with noise from the children, environment or poor acoustics – find another way to be 'heard'.

> **Do** keep hydrated and rest your voice whenever an opportunity occurs.

> **Respect your voice** – it is a valuable resource that can easily be damaged.

Planning individual music sessions

The ethos and structure of music and singing sessions will depend upon the age and characteristics of the children involved. The following is a rough guide:

♩ 0–2 years: informal, spontaneous singing woven into interactions and play.

♩ 2–3 years old: playful, enjoyable group singing.

♩ 4 years old: becoming more structured and consciously organised to build on the child's prior experience and spontaneous learning.

For each session it is necessary to identify appropriate learning objectives and to plan, in some detail, a variety of singing and movement activities to support children's musical progression towards these objectives.

Session features

1. Establish 'musical bookends' to start and end the session, to structure and define the time for music (e.g. *Hello/Goodbye* or start/end songs).

2. Ratio of rhymes to songs: in general, the younger the children, the higher the number of rhymes, 50:50 for the youngest age group with the number of songs over rhymes increasing as skills develop.

3. Vary the nature of the activities within the session to maintain concentration and enjoyment.

Alternate between:

o sitting, standing and moving, and utilise different physical areas of the room where possible

o individual role activities with ones requiring active, whole group participation. Involve the whole group as much as possible and avoid sitting for too long.

4. Include a musical *listening* activity, such as a parent playing an instrument or singing a song from another culture. Discuss the experience – it is important that children develop their listening and appraisal skills.

5. Plan for the most concentrated learning (i.e. the main musical objective) to be near the start of the session when the children's attention is likely to be most focused. Choose songs/rhymes to achieve a specific aim, not just because you like the song or the associated resource.

6. Repetition, repetition, repetition – both within the session and over a sequence of sessions. Repeat each song within a session, singing it continuously several times without stopping. Repeat over a number of *consecutive* sessions to build familiarity and extend learning; the more thoroughly the children know the song, the more you can do with it and the more layers of learning can be added.

7. Link songs and/or rhymes together (with the learning objective in mind) to aid continuity and spark children's interest. Make connections with topic areas, physical locations, stories, books or resources to extend musical and singing activities beyond the group session into the wider environment, continuous provision and home.

Check your plan: do the songs/rhymes and the associated activities fulfil the criteria set out by your aims and objectives?

In general:

➢ Think about the group concerned – e.g. class size, developmental level, individual children's additional needs (disability, language/ communication), etc. – and organise the songs, activities and resources, including additional supporting adults, accordingly.

➢ Plan for the class average including some tasks for the more able and some for the less able children. It is important that all the children have a positive experience and feel able to succeed.

➢ When planning make sure that the assessment process is considered and built in a practical and relevant manner. How will children's learning and progress be identified? How will this information be used?

➤ Be conscious of the individuality of children. Relating an action, puppet or topic area to a child's recent experience or interest could be key to them joining in and enjoying the song. However, the reverse is also true: a child who is terrified of puppets may well be put off music and singing by the resources you use.

➤ The children will participate more as singing becomes familiar and they develop their confidence and skills. This may mean that, initially, particularly with younger children, it is *you* that is doing most of the singing!

I have included two sample lesson plans for your information, one for a baby group with parents, the other for a preschool group in a nursery setting. There is no definitive 'one best way' to plan sessions and so these are offered purely as examples. Find the format that works best for you but ensure that all necessary information is included.

Session Plan 1: Children's centre baby group with parents

Objectives: singing and interaction with baby – to increase repertoire; experience of musical elements

Session no: 4

Song	Starting Pitch	Activity	Resources	Musical Element	Range
Hello! Hello! Hello! my friends, hello, hello to you Hello, hello to everyone, it's good to be with you[i] smsmsmrdsmsmrd smsmsmrdsmsmrd[ii]	A=so	Sing, sway and wave in time to steady beat	Puppet	Singing	smrd
<Name> where are you? **There you are, 'Hello' to you**[iii]	A=so	Hide under scarves – peepo to say 'Hello'	Scarves	Structure and timing Greeting individuals	sm
Make a circle[iv] [Action song]	F=do	Actions, some to steady beat, while carrying baby		Physical experience of steady beat, singing	mrd
Action rhyme	Rhyme	In circle; actions following words. Babies facing each other across the circle when jumping into the centre.		Steady beat with rest, structure	
Duck song	A=so	Actions with hands to steady beat.	Duck picture?	Listening, pulse	lsfmrd
Quack, quack, quack...		Voice play – duck speak conversation with hand 'quacking'		Interaction, humour	
Dancing song *Dance in pairs: parent holding baby facing another parent/child so that the babies are looking at each other*	A=so	Parent/baby pairs dancing with another parent/baby pair: Bow to each other, turn (changing places) as a couple facing each other.		Singing, phrasing, interaction	lsfmrd
Knee bob/riding game	Rhyme	Actions with baby on knees with lift and 'fall' at end.		Steady beat experience, pitch, anticipation, tempo	
Sea shells, sea shells, sing a song for me, Sing about the ocean, tell me about the sea s m s m f r rm s sm ms m fsfm rd	A=so	Row boat / sway / cuddle		Steady beat, pitch, listening and memory	sfmrd
Interactive rhyme with tickle and cuddle	Rhyme	Actions on baby to follow words		Anticipation, tempo, pitch, interaction	
Goodbye song	E=me	Tap legs and clap.		Steady beat, harmony – sing as a round	drms

i   Copyright Z Greenhalgh 2017.
ii Solfia included as aide memoir for melody (just in case!)
iii Bold typeface indicates this is a new song/rhyme for this group.
iv Words and Solfia removed for copyright reasons.

Session Plan 2: Nursery session with preschool children (aged 3–4 years)

Objectives: to sing with confidence at pitch; to consolidate sense of steady beat including rests (unconscious); to listen and respond

Week no: 3

Song	Starting Pitch	Activity	Resources	Musical Element	Tone set
Hello! Hello! Hello! my friends, hello, hello to you Hello, hello to everyone, it's good to be with you[i] smsmsmrdsmsmrd smsmsmrdsmsmrd	A=so	Sing, sway, wave (showing pitch contour) to steady beat		Singing, relative pitch, steady beat	lsmd
Copy cat song[ii] <solfa>	A=so	Sing solo & demonstrate action. Everyone copies & sings for 2nd time Child sings solo to show their chosen action, group watches then whole group echos.		Solo singing, pitch matching confidence	lsm
I saw Esau sitting on a see-saw I saw Esau he saw me I saw Esau sitting on a see-saw I saw Esau 1....2.....3![iii]	Rhyme	Clap and tap with a partner (standing)		Steady beat, coordination, team work (ensemble)	
<Words to pancake song> <solfa>	A=so	Make pancake – actions with hands; stir to steady beat, fry & toss Catch in rest at end **Catch 'pancake' on rest – clap & say topping (4 beats); group echos[iv]**	Bean bag	Singing, form and structure – rest, timing Preparation for rhythm	lsmd
Action rhyme	Rhyme	Perform actions standing in a circle. Miss out words		Steady beat with rest, inner hearing, coordination	
Swing me over the water, swing me over the sea Swing me over the garden wall and swing me home to tea s smmms s smmms sm s smmms sm ms sm md	A=so	Waft lycra up and down with fish toy on top. Sing 3 times then toss - 1, 2, 3, wee!	Rainbow lycra & fish	Singing, higher & lower pitch	smd
Goodbye <name>. Goodbye Zoe smsm	A=so	Echo response with hand movements to 4 steady beats: chest knee chest knee		Solo singing, listening, pitch matching	sm

Lesson plans are there to help and guide, not as a straightjacket.

Teacher's perspective = conscious, directed effort throughout

☺ **Child's perspective = engaging, joyful, playful** ☺

Planning for music in the wider environment and continuous provision

When planning group music activities think about ways to extend their impact into the children's independent learning and play opportunities. A story, resource or activity that becomes associated with a song or rhyme during group activities can then be used in the wider environment to trigger children's memory and inspire spontaneous singing and instrument exploration. For example, a song about chopping up food could be transferred to: the snack table, a cooking activity, playdough, the home corner, sand pit, a story containing fruit, vegetables or meal preparation, harvesting a crop, and so on. Activities modelled and experienced as a group activity can then be repeated, explored and extended independently by the children.

Present music activities in the same attractive and considered way as those supporting other areas of learning. Why not have a music table along with small world, mark making, etc.? The children can then see the resources and/or instruments laid out ready for them to explore and create.

Working with parents

Your attitude and response to parents will affect their level of participation and enjoyment. It is very important to be non-judgemental: there are many diverse cultural and childrearing practices which are all equally valid.

What can we do to encourage parents to participate?

Familiar songs and rhymes are often a helpful place to start. Information about what music and singing happens at home with parents, siblings and extended family members will be useful to identify family favourites, including music from other cultures.

♪ Create a friendly, relaxed and welcoming environment.

♪ Consider the size of the group, neither too big nor too small.

♪ When speaking to parents treat them as adults, equals and partners – value their input.

♪ If possible, include some time for parents to socialise. Parents of young children can feel very isolated.

♪ Manage expectations by giving parents sufficient information, particularly at the very beginning, so that they know what to expect and, perhaps more to the point, what you expect from them.

♪ Make sure the children and adults can access the activities. For example, an adult might not be able to sit on the floor or lift their child. Think creatively – there is always a solution.

♪ Establish a 'nurturing' atmosphere within the group where every participant is respected and failure is impossible.

♪ Plan carefully –

   o include familiar songs and rhymes to foster confidence

   o use lots of repetition to aid memory

   o think about the songs you choose – if they are achievable for the children they are also easier for the adults to sing. Remember, the more achievable the song, the more confident the singer and the more likely they are to join in – a positive cycle.

♪ Produce word sheets, linked resources or story books to encourage singing at home: for example a laminated, illustrated song sheet to go on the fridge, or a song sack with a linked activity, instrument and/or resource.

Above all, make the experience positive and enjoyable for all.

Planning a music curriculum
...a carefully thought-out plan to support progressive musical learning

Identify realistic and achievable aims for the year, *then* write the year plan/scheme of work. Think about what you want the children to achieve. These aims provide the basis for *all* planning and will combine to form a progressive, longer-term vision for the development of the children's musical learning.

Yearly plan (scheme of work)

Having identified the aims for the year, the scheme of work provides details of:

a) the songs, rhymes and musical tasks selected

b) an overview of how they will be developed to ensure progression

c) how progress will be assessed.

The resulting sequence, carefully thought out, will unfold over time, enabling each musical skill to be experienced and consolidated by each child. This will:

♩ ensure sequential development of children's skills

♩ progress the children's learning using small, logical and achievable steps, moving from simple objectives to more difficult activities

♩ build new knowledge upon prior learning. Children like what they already know so revisiting a *known* song for a *new* purpose is a good way to embark on a new area of learning. This embeds prior learning and makes the new skill more achievable as one element is already familiar to the child. Everyone enjoys the repetition of a well-loved song!

♩ ensure that any sequence of lessons has continuity.

Bear in mind that the children's musical development during this year is a part of a longer learning trajectory and cannot be viewed in isolation. Taking the children's prior musical learning and/or experience into account is therefore necessary.

How many songs?

Over the course of the year, the maximum number of *new* songs and rhymes that should be introduced has been suggested to be (Forrai 1998):

Age	Up to 3 years	3-4 years	5-6 years
Number of new songs/rhymes	20	24	30

At the beginning of each new term or block of sessions, it is helpful to repeat material that the children know from previous learning. This inspires confidence in the children by providing something familiar when class and/or social groupings may have changed. It also offers you the opportunity to assess their learning needs and plan accordingly.

Assessment

Planning and delivery are only part of the story! The effectiveness of the curriculum also needs to be assessed a) in terms of the children's learning, and b) to inform future planning and provision.

♩ Did the children learn what they were supposed to learn?

♩ If not, why not?

♩ What changes need to be made to the curriculum?

This assessment process takes place both in the moment, i.e. while the session is happening, and afterwards, looking back on what has occurred.

Observing children's participation and learning

Observation is vital for the assessment of children's learning and to facilitate reflective evaluation. Much of the assessment of children's learning will be gained through observation, particularly with the youngest, pre-verbal children. As leader, therefore, it is important to note and question even the smallest detail of each child's behaviour: rich and valuable information can be gleaned in this way about the quality of the child's experience and their learning journey.

Frameworks for observation (Young 2003; Pound and Harrison 2003)

When observing, consider the child's:

♩ participation in songs, both singing and learning them

♩ individual ability to reproduce the songs that they are learning

♩ participation in instrumental activity

♩ ability to reproduce rhythmic movements modelled for them

♩ ability to sing at pitch, in tune and solo.

Is the child:

♩ fully engaged

♩ partially engaged

♩ differently engaged, i.e. not as expected

♩ not engaged

♩ being coerced into participating?

Ask yourself why this is the case. For example, is it due to the environment, teaching style, the influence of other adults, etc.?

Reflective evaluation

There is, however, another important question to be asked when evaluating an individual session, programme or curriculum:

♩ What areas of personal practice do you, the leader, need to develop in terms of subject knowledge or pedagogy?

This question requires personal reflective evaluation, a valuable skill to acquire:

> *Learning to become a truly reflective practitioner is like being a butterfly – the metamorphosis may hurt as new thinking often requires change – but this will result in a more advanced state: flying rather than crawling: professional understanding rather than just technical application!*
>
> (Brock 2015, p. 9)

This activity can be broken down into stages which inform future planning but also acknowledge the importance of reflection by practitioners for their own professional development and learning, as well as informing future planning. In thinking about and analysing our work, we identify the strengths and weaknesses in our practice, prompting us to extend our knowledge and skills and 'up our game' – which leads us back to the notion of Kaizen as mentioned earlier in this book – the pursuit of constant improvement.

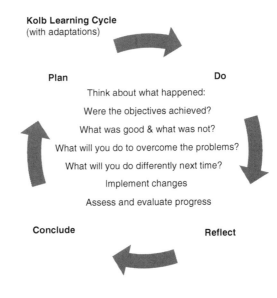

Kolb Learning Cycle
(with adaptations)

Plan   **Do**

Think about what happened:
Were the objectives achieved?
What was good & what was not?
What will you do to overcome the problems?
What will you do differently next time?
Implement changes
Assess and evaluate progress

Conclude   **Reflect**

Time spent on devising well-thought-out, clearly articulated plans is time very well spent and will impact on both the quality of sessions and on the children's progression. Well planned sessions are so much easier and satisfying to deliver. There is much truth in the old adage 'Fail to prepare, prepare to fail'!

References

Brock, A. 2015. What is reflection and reflective practice? In Brock, A. *The Early Years Reflective Practice Handbook*. Abingdon: Routledge.

Forrai, K. 1998. *Music in Pre-School*. Brisbane: Clayfield School of Music.

Pound, L. and Harrison, C. 2003. *Supporting Musical Development in the Early Years*. Buckingham: Oxford University Press.

Young, S. 2003. *Music with the Under-Fours*. London: RoutledgeFalmer.

6 | Putting the planning into practice

As already mentioned within the pages of this book, songs and rhymes need to be chosen with care. Start with very simple songs and rhymes. Remember, do not try to make the children run before they can walk; firmly establish the basics of pitch and steady beat before moving on.

Songs and rhymes and their associated activities obviously need to be appropriate, *but the leader also needs to like them*. The children are *never* going to find a song you dislike as attractive as one you enjoy singing.

If you lack confidence in singing, these simple songs will help you to improve and learn along with the children. Find a way to help you – if you have a child or colleague who sings very well, ask them to model songs, or try using one of the many digital apps available to support your learning.

If *you* find a song hard to sing, young children probably will too. So, remember to consider the following:

1. How complex is the melody to sing?

To help them learn to control their voices and sing accurately, young children need to start with songs which use very few pitches, i.e. two or three. Compare the nursery rhyme 'Humpty Dumpty' with 'Rain, rain go away'. Which one is harder to sing well? 'Humpty Dumpty' has a huge range of pitches from low to very high with some very tricky bits of melody in between. 'Rain, rain go away' has two or three pitches (depending on the tune you know) and is considerably easier *for you* to sing as well as being an appropriate starting point for developing the *accuracy* of young children's singing.

Choose simple songs with a limited range of pitches:

♩ Two pitches: as in a 'cuckoo' call

  o Solfa = s-m; interval = falling minor 3rd; e.g. pitch names = A to F#

♩ Three pitches: as in the ubiquitous playgroup chant 'na na na na na'

  o Solfa = s m l s m; e.g. pitch names = A F#BA F#

  or 'Three Blind Mice'

  o Solfa = m r d; e.g. pitch names = F# E D

♩ Gradually progress to five-note pentatonic scale (i.e. penta = 5, tonic = note)

  o Solfa = l s m r d; e.g. pitch names = B A F#E D; range = major 6th

This scale has no semitones or half steps which are harder to pitch. The 'black' notes on a piano keyboard make up a pentatonic scale.

A series of descending pitches is easier to sing in tune than an ascending series and consecutive notes are easier than jumps.

Remember!

What adults like to sing is not necessarily what children like. You may have reservations about using such simple songs, but the children will not. They will happily sing and learn from them again and again.

2. How difficult are the words to say?

How many syllables are there in each line? Children will learn more easily if the words are easy to hear and say. Repetition within the rhyme/song is also helpful.

♩ Is there more than one note to a syllable? One note to a syllable makes it easier to hear the phonetic sounds of the words. This encourages the child to reproduce these sounds accurately, thereby aiding language development and future literacy skills.

♩ Simple rhymes/songs are usually more flexible and multi-purpose. Once they are known well the activity can be altered to increase complexity and deepen learning.

3. How many different note lengths are there?

As discussed in the rhythm section two note lengths within the song is generally the optimum that this age group can accurately reproduce, e.g. ♩ ♫. These relate to the rhythms of the child's everyday life; i.e. walking ♩ and running ♫.

♩ Simple rhythms are best to begin with, increasing in complexity step by step as appropriate to the learning of each individual group of children.

4. Is the song 'fit for purpose'?

What do you want to achieve with a particular song or rhyme? What is the objective? Will the way you have planned to use it achieve this objective?

♩ Decide on the aim of the activity *first*, and then choose the song or rhyme to achieve this goal.

♩ Is it appropriate for the age group/developmental level of the children in terms of the song features and the associated actions or game?

♩ Is what you are asking the children to do achievable?

Checklist – 10 points for successful delivery

1. *Know your material well.*

Fail to prepare, prepare to fail.

Learn the song/rhyme well and practise singing it from memory, along with the associated actions. Decide in advance *why* and *how* you are going to use the song and *what* you want the children to do. The children will copy your example, warts and all, so the better your performance in front of the children, the better the final result will be!!

2. *Provide a good example.*

Think about your presentation of the song/rhyme.

♩ Use appropriate pitch. Find a way *for you* to identify a suitable starting pitch by using a chime bar, recorder, tuning fork, digital app – whatever works best for you. Please note that most young children can only pitch accurately from a *sung* note and will need to take the pitch from a voice.

♩ Sing the song as accurately and as musically as possible, especially the first time the children hear it as this will help to stimulate their interest. Use your voice, face and body expressively. Pronounce the words clearly with good diction. With rhymes use melodious speech which is full of expression and contrasting pitches.

   o Be rhythmically accurate. Keep a steady beat – do not speed up or slow down. Remember – the steady beat continues through any rests which may occur in the middle or right at the end.

   o Tap steady beat on legs, clap the rhythm, to differentiate between these two concepts. Perform all actions accurately and in time.

   o Perform rhymes rhythmically and expressively, using the pattern of the words.

   o Ensure other adults provide a good role model. In addition, give them a 'turn' to provide an example for the children to copy. It is much more effective to model the game or response than to try to explain it.

3. How fast?

The optimum speed is probably slower than you think!

The tempo has to be slow enough for the children to hear each *syllable* and *pitch* clearly enough to be able to reproduce it accurately. Generally, the younger the child the slower the tempo, especially with new material.

♪ Listen to the children's responses and adjust the tempo as necessary.

♪ Once a rhyme/song is known *well* play with it; for example, varying the tempo or using pauses to increase anticipation of the punchline.

4. Don't sing too loudly.

Young children's singing voices are not very loud.

Try to sing *with* the children rather than *at* them. Use a *singing together* approach where all voices are heard equally rather than the leader's voice being dominant.

♪ If you sing loudly the children may shout rather than sing, or they may stop joining in at all as their voices are overwhelmed. Singing *with* the children enables you to hear their voices.

♪ If possible, drop out now and then and listen so that you can hear the quality of the singing and give your own voice a rest.

5. Use movement.

Rhythmic movement not only adds interest to the song/rhyme, it also increases its impact. Movement:

♪ enhances the child's gross and fine motor skills by stimulating the nervous system and developing coordination. Make sure you alternate left- and right-sided movements to stimulate both sides of the body and brain equally.

♪ increases memory by adding another sensory dimension to the experience, creating muscular memories and images in the brain.

♪ reinforces the steady beat, rhythm, structure or pitch contour of the song. These movements also make the child's learning visible, thus enabling the leader to assess progression.

Clapping a steady beat is easier than walking it; the further away from the brain, the harder it is to control movement with accuracy. Children have shorter arms and legs than adults and will therefore naturally clap, walk or use a beater at a slightly faster speed than more long-limbed grown-ups. It is important to choose a tempo that is 'child-friendly' to make success as easy as possible.

Another way to help with movement in time to a steady beat is to ask the child to start moving first; then the song can be sung in time to the child's actions. Once the child has experienced how it feels to move in time it is easier for them to reproduce it at will.

♩ As leader, use big continuous motions (with body or beaters). This makes your modelling clearer but also symbolises that music is never static, even during rests. A piece of music is continuous from beginning to end. For example, imagine a bouncing ball: the 'bounce' represents the steady beat, but the ball continues to move between bounces. When keeping a steady beat, larger motions will also discourage children from adding unrequired movements between beats, particularly when the tempo is slower.

♩ Try to avoid actions that are so complicated or difficult to perform that they impact on the child's ability to sing successfully and/or distract their attention away from your intended objective.

♩ Be aware that slow is hard!

6. *Think about your verbal and non-verbal prompts.*

Find what works for you and the children you work with.

♩ Present singing as a very 'normal' activity, spontaneous and informal. Show that you enjoy singing and are having a good time and that it is not just another thing you need to teach.

♩ Speak as little as possible and just 'do' – the children will join in; you will save time and find it easier to keep the children's attention.

Remember!

I see and I forget
I hear and I believe
I do and I understand (Confucius)

♩ Sing instructions, for example:

o *'Stand up'*: two pitches – lower to higher (e.g. the first two pitches of 'Twinkle Twinkle Little Star' = d-s)

o *'Sit down'*: the same two pitches in reverse – higher to lower (i.e. s-d)

o *'Sit down on the carpet...'*, etc.

If you are consistent with the tunes for each instruction, after time you could drop the words and just sing the melody – a great game to play!

♩ How are you going to lead the group into the song/rhyme? Experiment and find out what works best for you. One way is to sing something like 'Are you read-y?' over four beats on the song's starting pitch, or to the tune of the first line. This may be helpful to encourage everyone to start together, but be mindful that with very young children it can reduce a joyful song or game to a much less attractive 'taught lesson'. In my experience, the youngest children usually join you in singing this introduction, making it a pointless exercise!

♩ Think about your movements and body language. Are they clear and positive? Are you modelling what you want to see? Do you look as if you're enjoying yourself?

7. Repeat as many times as possible.

Children enjoy singing songs and rhymes that they know well and they learn by repeating things again and again. Do not be afraid to sing a song or rhyme several times without stopping. Be inventive and play – think of ways to repeat your material many times in one sitting. This enables the children to become familiar with it and work up the confidence to join in. Simple ideas are often the best – the possibilities are endless. Here are a few ideas for keeping repetition interesting:

♩ Ask children to do actions with a teddy. Swap teddies and do it again.

♩ The child does the actions with a partner, e.g. 'row' a boat, clap and tap hands, roll a ball, dance, etc. Swap partners and repeat.

♩ Change the activity, e.g. stand instead of sit, introduce a resource (puppet or instrument) to maintain interest and/or progress learning.

♩ Take turns to play the steady beat, rhythm or ostinato (short repeated rhythmic pattern) on an instrument to add an accompaniment to the song.

♩ Use different 'voices', e.g. whisper, shout, robot, fairy, story character, tired, cross, etc.

♩ Insert the child's name into the song/rhyme

Children's musical potential thrives on experience.
(Young, S. 2009, p. 15)

8. Be positive and playful.

Children learn best when they are enjoying themselves, and they are more likely to be involved and interested if they see that you are enjoying the activities too.

♩ Sing spontaneously and frequently. For example, sing instructions; play with your voice, making sounds to accompany stories, movement, children's play, etc.; sing anything and everything, whatever comes into your head in any way you fancy. The children will be enchanted by such playfulness, and it adds another dimension to life!

♩ Maintain eye contact with the children; connect and communicate. Be playful and creative together. Be spontaneous and be prepared (if appropriate) to abandon your plan and follow the children's lead.

♩ **Never** underestimate what a child can do: *'what we expect from children is what we get'* (Young 2009, p. 87).

♩ **Create a nurturing environment where children, parents/carers and staff all feel safe to participate and take risks. Value all contributions.**

♩ **Never** force an activity on a child. It is OK for children to watch and listen from a distance.

♩ **Keep communication positive** – there is no *'right'* or *'wrong'*, only *'variations'*. Ban the use of *'No'* and *'shhh'*. Instead try 'Have another go'.

♩ Take note: when a child does not respond as expected it is usually as a result of unclear instructions or the introduction of an inappropriate next step.

♩ When asking a question, ask the group as a whole rather than putting pressure on one individual child. No response? No problem! **Create a culture where failure is impossible.**

♩ Do not laugh, and discourage others from laughing, when a child does something sweet, charming, unexpected or funny. This can be devastating for the child's self-esteem if they think they are being laughed *at*, and they may be very reluctant to join in with activities again.

♩ Do not make too big an issue of anything that may form a barrier between the child and musical activities. Take care to always 'leave the door open' so that the child feels that they are welcome to join in when they feel able to do so.

9. *Use of instruments.*

Think about what you want to achieve. If the whole group plays an instrument, will they still be able to hear the song, and will *you* be able to hear anything of value? Asking just one or two children to play adds a new dimension to a known song and is less intrusive to the activity. It also offers you the opportunity to assess the child's progress and provides a great excuse to repeat the activity a number of times, to deepen learning and give more children a turn.

10. *Evaluate and adjust both during and after.*

Think about how well your activities are/were received and make any adjustments that might improve the children's experience.

♩ What was good and what was not? Why? Could you make it better? If not, what could?

♩ Do not 'flog a dead horse'. Pick up cues from the children and move on when their interest wanes.

♩ Repeat the activity if the children are enjoying it, but be mindful to leave them wanting more!

♩ Reflect upon your teaching and musical skills. Acknowledge what you do well and seek opportunities for professional development to improve weaker areas.

Reference

Young, S. 2009. *Music 3–5*. London: RoutledgeFalmer.

7 | Resources for music making

'**What's in your bag?**' is probably the question I am asked most frequently during training workshops so I thought it would be useful to include a chapter on resources and how they might be used.

So, in my bag there is:

♪ a piece of Lycra

♪ a square of star fabric

♪ a soft toy (fish)

♪ a hand puppet

♪ a bag of finger puppets

♪ two pop-up puppets (one full size, one small)

♪ a magic wand, book and box

♪ a soft ball

♪ a descant recorder

♪ a couple of pairs of claves

♪ jingle bells

♪ a castanet

♪ a Talking Point voice recording device.

In general I believe that as far as your resources are concerned the quality of their sound, feel and texture is equally as important as their appearance. And it goes without saying that treating these items with respect encourages the children to do the same. The way you store your resources also contributes to this; for instance, using colourful fabric bags rather than plastic carrier bags makes them far more interesting to the children as their contents cannot be seen until the bag is opened, adding to the sense of anticipation.

Lycra

This is the stretchy material used to make dance and sportswear. It comes in a huge variety of colours and patterns and is widely available on the internet and in fabric shops.

A length of 1.5 metres provides a square of fabric which can accommodate up to approximately 20 children, either all sitting or all standing around the edge holding the edge with both hands. This can be used in any number of ways. Here are a few ideas:

♩ With a soft toy on the top

The children work together as a team, controlling the Lycra (e.g. in time to the steady beat and/or following the melody line), synchronising their movements and maintaining their self-control so that the toy bounces as required. This demands of each child a great awareness of the whole group, to actively listen, watch and work as part of the team to achieve their common goal. Ways of using the Lycra include:

o moving the Lycra up and down or side to side,

o constant shallow and controlled bouncing of the soft toy,

o a 'pull and release' motion using the elasticity of the fabric, i.e. all children rocking backwards at the same time so that the fabric is stretched, then rocking forwards together to release this tension,

throughout, until the climax of the song, when the toy is tossed into the air. The better the team work, the higher the toy jumps!

♩ Choosing an individual child

The direction in which the soft toy bounces may provide a way of choosing which child will next participate within the activity by offering an idea, choosing a colour or taking a turn playing an instrument for example.

♩ A child underneath the Lycra

There are several ways that this can work.

- o The child beneath the Lycra plays an instrument to provide additional accompaniment to the song: for example, in a song about the sea, it could be a wave drum to suggest the sound of the waves.

- o At specific points in the song the child uses her body to stretch the fabric by 'popping up' like a jack-in-a-box. This requires the child to understand the structure of the song/rhyme, anticipating and coordinating her responses in order to move at the appropriate moment. A single-colour Lycra piece is particularly effective for this type of activity as it moulds to the shape of the child's head, face and hands, providing much enjoyment and rich conversation from the main group of children watching from around the edge of the fabric.

- o One child or more beneath the fabric might respond to music or song in a freestyle, creative and individual way by making shapes and/or movements against the taut Lycra, such as finger-pinching to represent a crab's claws or using the edge of an outstretched hand to form a shark's fin. If the children have bare feet and sit with legs straight out in front of them, their toes can clearly be seen and wiggling them can be a vehicle for much play, humour and conversation.

♩ Holey Lycra

Using a piece of Lycra with holes cut into it allows for much playfulness (Arculus ND), extending the possibilities for children's creative interactions both with, and through, the Lycra, such as: looking through the holes to the other side, poking fingers/hands/feet/finger

Source: St Peter's Primary Preschool, Budleigh Salterton. R. Tomlinson – Take Art Ltd.

puppets/toys through the holes, or threading scarves in and out. This provides much opportunity for playful, non-verbal communication using vocalisations and movement to accompany actions.

In addition to Lycra, other types of fabric can be used in many creative ways. Saris, which are bought in a fixed length, are often inexpensive and available in a stunning range of colours, patterns and textures. Here are some ideas for using saris and other fabric pieces.

♩ Babies and young toddlers love to lie on the floor looking up at the pattern on pieces of fabric. For example, a pieces of fabric printed with small shiny coloured stars can be 'wafted' gently over them while everyone sings 'Twinkle Twinkle Little Star' several times without pause. It is even better if those singing can add a little harmony along the way!

♩ Arrange several saris (one person holding each end) in a star formation, above infants lying on their backs looking upwards. While singing a lullaby, repeatedly raise all the saris together and allow them to float gently downwards in time with the phrasing of the song. This creates a calming and visually interesting experience that is truly beautiful.

♩ A sari or long length of fabric makes an excellent boat/bus/train, etc. Seat the children in a line, one in front of another down the middle of the length of fabric, all facing the same direction. Each child holds the two side edges of the fabric, one in each hand, bringing it upwards and in towards their bodies to form a boat-like shape.

♩ A length of fabric can also represent a song feature: for example, a blue sari arranged on the floor can be a stream over which the children jump back and forth to the steady beat while singing a related song. Many other resources can also be used this way: e.g. a crack in the paving outside, the edge of the carpet or grass, a rope or line of sand – the possibilities are endless!

♩ There are many hiding songs/games that can be played in a group using a large piece of fabric. However, it is worth highlighting the point that some children are not confident at hiding beneath or behind something when they cannot see what is happening on the other side. Therefore, patterned fabric *through which the child can see* is useful. The child doing the hiding can see what is happening 'outside' and so feel safer but, because of the pattern, the children around them cannot easily identify the child underneath.

♩ Small square scarves can be used for babies and toddlers to hide behind and play *Peepo*. A short simple song which has a 'peepo' punchline (where the scarf is removed) enables the group to greet and acknowledge each individual by name. As always, some form of physical motion in relation to the steady beat is recommended to accompany the song, such as hand movements, swaying gently or rocking a babe-in-arms. This activity provides a physical experience of the song's form and structure, embedding additional knowledge of the song in the child's memory – how long it is and where the punchline occurs – so that after a number of repetitions, the child is able to anticipate the end and remove the scarf himself with precision timing and great satisfaction!

Puppets – hand puppet, finger puppets, pop-up puppet

Puppets of various types and sizes can be used to great effect when singing with young children. The first few years of life are a magical time when the boundaries of reality can be blurred, allowing for much joyful, rich and creative experience. Used well, puppets (and soft toys) can contribute to this by being 'alive' and providing a conduit though which a child can communicate and play. To be successful this 'magic' needs to be maintained with the puppet being presented and behaving as an autonomous being and the adults joining the children in total complicit acceptance of this illusion. When manipulating a puppet it is therefore vital that we appear unconnected, responding to it as a separate being worthy of our focused attention as if we do not know what will happen next. Joining in and 'playing the game' in this way draws the children in, inviting their attention both as individuals and as a group. Thus roles are blurred, with the leader becoming one of the group and the puppet recognised as the one 'in charge'. To maintain this pretence, it is important that the puppet is not available for the children to play with independently – it lives where it lives and only comes out at particular times, i.e. totally under the control of the leader.

There is always one child who swims against the tide and declares – vocally! – something along the lines of 'that's not real, it's only a puppet!' The best response I have seen to this comes from Lucinda Geoghegan, Education Consultant at National Youth Choir of Scotland, who swiftly covers the ears of the puppet and exclaims to the children, 'I know that, you know that, but <the puppet> doesn't!'

Remember!

Not all children like puppets – some children find them very scary and such resources should therefore be introduced gently while you observe the response of each individual child. We must be sensitive to all children's fears and feelings and there is *always* an alternative way to achieve the same learning experience.

Use of hand puppets

It is often the case that a young child feels more comfortable communicating with a puppet than with an adult, making a skilfully presented puppet a valuable tool, a situation I experienced during a recent project:

> *Hassan, a 2-year-old boy, had never been heard to speak in his nursery setting and there was concern about his language acquisition. Flossy, the lemur hand puppet, lives and sleeps in my bag, snoring frequently. I was with Hassan with another child looking on. There was much anticipation as I tried to rouse Flossy from her slumbers and encourage her to come out to meet him. I sang 'Wake up Flossy' several times; the snoring stopped and something moved in the bag. Eventually, she woke up and slowly came out to say hello. Hassan had been completely absorbed in listening and watching what was happening. When Flossy finally emerged, he was totally entranced; he grasped her paws in his hands, looked deep into her eyes and spoke to her, and her alone, continuously for several minutes.*

Finger puppets

A child who is reluctant to sing or talk may feel able to respond without inhibitions through the medium of a puppet, singing a response using the puppet's 'voice' rather than her own. Giving each child a finger puppet and singing to the *puppet* rather than to the child directs any sense of expectation and attention towards the puppet instead of the child. Ideas for ways to use finger puppets to encourage solo singing can be found in Chapter 2.

Having a wide variety of finger puppets in your collection is useful as it allows all children to find one that suits their particular interests: animal, dinosaur, helicopter, fish, fairy, flower, etc. It is very important that the puppets used are the right length to fit the finger of a small child and, of course, that they are safe for a young child to play with.

Tip: Putting finger puppets or other resources back into the bag at the end of the activity tends to be time consuming and children's interest can easily be lost. Having a 'putting away' ritual is therefore helpful and can still serve a musical learning objective; for example, while singing a particular song the children place their puppets in the bag as it is passed around the circle; the song ends with the leader closing the bag in a playful, engaging way. I play a game with the zip of the bag, making an ascending 'zzzzzzz' sound as I close it bit by bit, in short bursts, building anticipation for the final stretch which closes the bag completely. The children are always agog, joining in with the sound-making and movements, keenly awaiting the climax when the zip is finally closed. This is a ritual that has developed over time while working with children and is specific to putting things away. Interestingly I have great difficulty recalling the song in isolation from the activity!

Use of a specific puppet (or puppets) within a story or song can serve as an effective visual prompt for the story subject. The puppet will then also by default become associated with that story/song/activity and be used to stimulate independent exploration within the wider continuous provision. It is here that the child has the opportunity and freedom to play, to develop and extend the activity, to re-sequence component parts, to try out new ideas, improvise and compose.

Pop-up puppet

Pop-up puppets are a highly versatile and useful resource. They can be used:

♩ to conduct the group, serving as a focal point to demonstrate when to start, how fast, etc.

♩ to encourage solo singing by popping up when sung to

♩ to show the form and structure of songs and rhymes

♩ to indicate dynamic change (louder/quieter)

♩ in the development of inner hearing (thinking voice).

These techniques are discussed in Chapters 2 and 3.

Magic

Magic is a joy to use. It entrances children completely and most are desperate to see more and have a turn. You will be delighted to know that membership of the Magic Circle is not required, as commercially available resources – magic box, magic book – are more than adequate! You will need to practise, however, in order to convince the children that the 'magic' wand they are holding is indeed capable of real magic! The leader however must retain full control of the magic book or box to maintain the mystery.

Magical resources can be used in much the same way as a pop-up puppet, e.g. to encourage solo singing or the accuracy of singing with slightly older children. They are also useful however in developing a child's rhythmic understanding and skill, e.g. tapping the steady beat or rhythm on the book/box with the magic wand while singing the song, followed by their chosen magic word. When the 'magic' happens, in an awe-inspiring 'Wow!' moment, it is accompanied by a huge sense of achievement for the wand waver. This can be a transformative experience for some children, boosting their self-confidence.

The rest of the children in the group can be practising alongside, using their personal 'magic wands' – tapping the forefinger of one hand on the upturned open palm of the other hand. This ensures that all the children are not only involved but repeat the activity multiple times, thereby reinforcing the learning even when it is another child's turn to wave the wand.

Remember!

Below a certain age, magic is not at all wondrous. In the life of a small child things are constantly appearing and disappearing without explanation, thus making magic very unremarkable! Using these resources is therefore most effective with children from around three and a half to four years of age.

Soft ball

There are a number of songs which involve rolling a ball to a child for them to roll back. This motion can be used as an activity to acknowledge each child personally at the start of the session or day or to learn names at the start of a new term or year. Some songs offer the opportunity for the child to sing a solo response and, because everyone is concentrating on the ball, children are often comfortable enough to sing this spontaneously without even realising it. No response, no problem. Making no comment or issue about it leaves the opportunity open for the child to react to the ball sometime in the future.

A soft ball is preferable to a hard, bouncy ball as it is easier to control and easier for small hands to manipulate. I use one that is about the same size as a large orange.

Recorder

As discussed in an earlier chapter, young children need much experience and exposure to music from sources other than the human voice in order to develop their awareness of pitch and timbre. Playing without any introduction – on a recorder or other instrument – a song which the children sing and know really well is an interesting exercise in finding out whether they are able to identify which song it is. If you consistently sing classroom instructions such as *Stand up, Sit down*, etc. and the children are totally comfortable with directions given in this way, perhaps you might like to mix things up and challenge the children's listening skills by transferring these melodies to the recorder. I suspect you might instantly gain the children's complete attention!

Personally, I prefer not to let the children play my recorder, partly for hygiene reasons, partly because an overblown recorder at close quarters is not pleasant, but also because a group situation is not ideal for such an activity – every child wants a turn, and if they are one of the lucky ones who has a turn, it will be unsatisfactorily short! Exploring instruments takes time and should not be public or rushed. It is also imperative that children learn to treat musical instruments with respect and handle them with care. A recorder is reasonably robust, but a ukulele or clarinet is not and nor are many of the multicultural musical instruments found in many early years settings. And some instruments, particularly those played by visiting musicians, may be extremely valuable and it is vital that they are treated appropriately.

If you wish to introduce a blown instrument, four-holed ocarinas are a good alternative to the recorder. They have a more mellow tone, are easy to blow and play and, being made of plastic with no constituent parts, they are much easier to clean.

Witnessing someone play an instrument live is a multi-faceted experience, far removed from passively listening to a recording or watching video. It can exert a powerful effect on the children and is virtually guaranteed to grab their attention. This is partly due to the impact of the sound coming from the instrument itself and partly because that sound is being produced in front of their very eyes by someone they may know, and with whom they might have a close relationship.

Talk to the children, their parents and the staff. Find out if they know anyone in their family circle or community who can play an instrument and invite them in to play for the children. This not only provides a valuable musical experience but also presents positive role models to the children, demonstrating to them that many people play musical instruments and that it is something to which they too can aspire.

Claves

Claves are an untuned percussion instrument, essentially consisting of a couple of short wooden sticks played by tapping one upon the other. In early years music making they can be used in a seemingly limitless number of creative ways. For example:

♩ Used in the traditional way by tapping one upon the other to keep the steady beat, rhythm or an ostinato. This is more effective if there are only a very small number of children playing them at any one time so that the sounds they produce can be heard clearly and do not drown out the children's singing. The rest of the group can practise using their 'magic claves', i.e. each child tapping their pointing forefingers, one against the other.

♩ Finger puppets fit well onto the end of a clave and make an excellent 'tapper' for use on a hard surface, e.g. the floor or a wood block (see the figure on page 91). By transforming the clave into a dancing song-related character, tapping the steady beat, etc.

becomes a playful activity rather than a less imaginative, routine educational task.

There are many objects that can be used in this way, for example:

♩ Wooden spoons. To accompany a song about a girl called Mary-Ann who makes porridge my bag contains a couple of dressed wooden spoons – Mary-Ann and Stan the Man – who dance to the song (see the figure on page 92). Having two spoons means that the child can choose the one they prefer and the leader can use the other; thus the couple 'dance' together with the leader modelling the relevant movement (steady beat/ rhythm, etc.) for the child to copy if needed.

♩ Pencil toppers, i.e. unsharpened pencils with a character or object fused onto one end, also make good tappers and are available with a wide variety of interesting tops.

Odds and ends

These resources are not used as regularly as others and tend to be connected with specific activities.

The **castanet** is useful for 'dipping' rhymes (i.e. counting-out rhyme such as 'Eeny Meeny Miny Mo'), used to select an individual child from a group. Clicking with the castanet as each child is 'counted' emphasises the steady beat which, when coupled with a clear, emphatic movement, turns an essentially transitional task – choosing who has the next turn – into a focused game and a valuable opportunity for unconscious learning.

The **jingle bells** are used mainly for listening games where a blindfolded child has to work out who took the bells during a song.

Bean bags are used predominantly during singing games to represent an object, most commonly becoming:

♩ a dog's bone in a listening/guessing game, i.e. an object to identify a 'role' (dog or thief)

♩ a pancake to 'toss' to an adult or the leader, i.e. as a different way to mark a beat, rest or particular point in a song or rhyme. This takes skill as the child needs to anticipate the beat and throw the bag so that it lands *on* the beat. Bean bags are delightfully tactile and easy for small hands to handle and, when made from colourful, interesting fabric, are attractive to small children.

PVC-coated/vinyl table cloth is useful to provide children with ideas to enable them to contribute to an activity. For example, when singing a song about making a pie, a cloth covered in different types of fruit acts as a visual prompt, supporting the children in choosing a fruit filling for their pie. This cloth can then be used on the snack table or elsewhere in the environment, extending the usage of music activities into the wider continuous provision.

Floor spots

These make excellent puddles, stepping stones, pathways, etc. In musical terms they can be used:

♩ in combination with movement as a visual (preferably soundless) representation of a rest (silent beat) within a song, e.g. marking the rests in a song about rain by silently jumping in a puddle.

♩ to make the steady beat visible. In the first instance, unconscious musical learning can be fostered through use of the spots to frame the movement of the child by providing stepping stones to walk on in time to a steady beat. The way the spots are placed and the colour patterns used serves to show the structure of the song/rhyme, for example the number of beats in a line/phrase and the number of phrases in the song. In time and after much musical experience, this can be explained to the children and subsequently built upon to extend and progress musical learning, e.g. by using the same colour to represent identical lines within a song, or using varied colours to represent changes in pitch. In this way children can be introduced to the idea of visual representation of music as a precursor to notation.

Musical instruments

As previously discussed, musical instruments are used most effectively in early childhood through supported individual free play. This allows the child to explore and create without restriction in much the same way as in other areas of learning within the continuous provision, such as the construction area. Instruments can also be utilised to provide a different texture and/or timbre when used in very small numbers as an accompaniment to a song. In whatever way they are used it is important that the instruments:

a) make a good-quality sound. A few high-quality instruments are preferable to a large set of instruments that are out of tune, make an unmusical sound or are in a poor state of repair.

b) are playable by young children. This might require adapted beaters or simple stands to hold the instrument so that the child can play it successfully: e.g. using a table stand for a triangle or suspended cymbal.

c) are presented in a manner that both entices and enables the child to explore and create. When planning for music in the continuous provision, think about *where* you position the instruments. Louder instruments, for example, may be better outside. Setting instruments out with the same attention to detail as is usual with other continuous provision activities makes them much more visible and will attract the children's interest. Research suggests that *how* instruments are set out has an impact on the way in which the children respond and play them (Burke & Power 2014). For example, placing chime bars on a table means that children can play while standing and, as a result, are able to move more freely and expressively, using the whole body and large gestures. Movement is therefore an integral element of children's creative music making.

'Talking point' voice recorder

Small devices of this type record around 30 seconds of sound and are used by many nursery settings to support children's speech and language development. Simple to use and easily operated by the children themselves they can be used in many creative ways. For example:

♩ Record yourself singing a song and leave the device in the continuous provision along with associated resources/activities. This enables access to the song by the child on his terms, if and when he wants to hear it, providing a model rendition of the words/tune, etc. And, maybe, provoking a response.

♩ Record a child singing a song. Children love hearing their singing voice played back to them. Perhaps they could play it back to their parents at home time?

♩ Leave it with the associated resources, or in a designated 'singing space', so that children can record themselves singing whatever they fancy. This could provoke a whole host of lovely spontaneous singing from children who are perhaps less confident in a group situation. Children's own improvised songs may also be captured.

Many of these devices have the facility to place a picture on the top. This could be something which relates to the song in some way or to an individual child.

Other, more sophisticated child-friendly recording devices store multiple recordings which are downloadable via a USB connection to a computer. Perhaps these could be used in relation to an interactive whiteboard? Imagine, the child touches a picture on the board and hears her own voice singing a song! I am sure there are many imaginative ways of using such technology – a future project perhaps?

A myriad of lovely resources, of many types, are widely available – at times they can be irresistibly enticing as is clearly demonstrated by my bulging cupboard! At the end of the day, though, the best and most effective resource at your disposal is *you* – *your* relationship with the children, *your* knowledge and skill, and the way in which *you* go about doing what you do.

References

Arculus, C. (ND). Private communication.

Burke, N. and Power, T. 2014. *Enabling Musical Environments: An action research report*. London: Sound Connections. [Online] Available from: http://s587303541.websitehome.co.uk/wp-content/uploads/2016/06/N.Burke-T.Power-Musical-Environments.pdf [Accessed 29 September 2017].

Glossary

Compose: to consciously combine and manipulate musical elements to make a piece of music

Dynamic(s): relates to the volume of the music: louder and quieter

Ensemble: a group of individuals playing music or singing together as a group

Form and structure: the construction of a song or rhyme; the number of phrases (lines) used, their length and pattern, and any repetitions

Improvise: to sing or play music as a stream of consciousness; music that is made in the moment

Infant Directed Speech (motherese): speech at a higher than normal pitch, a 'sing-song' style of speech using short phrases with exaggerated, lengthened and repeated words

Inner hearing (thinking voice): the ability to 'sing' silently inside your head. Requires the development of musical (aural) memory

Interval: the distance between two different pitches

Intonation: the accuracy of pitching when singing or playing a musical instrument

Metre: the number of beats in a bar (e.g. a waltz = 3 beats, a march = 4 beats) identified in the time signature at the beginning of the written music

Mother tongue: the intonation and characteristics of the language an infant hears most from her early childhood home environment

Motherese: see Infant Directed Speech

Multi-modal: learning using several different ways of activity, e.g. singing+movement+interaction with others in a singing game

Notation: any form of symbolisation used to represent musical sound. Traditionally stave notation but pictures or objects can also be used

Pentatonic: penta = 5, tonic = note. A sequence of five notes with no semitones (half-tone intervals). The black notes of the piano keyboard form a pentatonic scale

Pitch: how high or low musical notes are heard due to the frequency (hertz) of the sound

Pitch matching: the ability to accurately reproduce a pitch that is sung by another. This requires the ability to hear the note and control the voice to reproduce it

Range: the interval between the lowest and highest pitches, e.g. within a song or phrase

Relative pitch: the exact relationship between notes/pitches, which enables 'singing in tune'

Rest: a silent beat or beats

Rhythm: irregular and changing, possibly with silent gaps (rests) – often the patterns made by the words in a song

Semitone: half of a tone (pitch-related)

Solfa:

i. Melodic – syllables and associated hand signs to represent the degrees of a musical scale, i.e. d r m f s l t d

ii. Rhythmic – syllables to represent rhythmic note duration, which enable rhythm to be verbalised accurately, e.g. ta, te, sh

Steady beat (Pulse): the 'heartbeat' of the music – how you would walk (march) to a song/rhyme. Features: regular and unchanging. Continues through silent beats right to the end of the song/rhyme. The foundation of all music. The ability to feel a steady beat is fundamental to all musical participation and the first skill that needs to be acquired.

Tempo: the speed of the music: faster or slower

Timbre: the 'flavour' of the individual sound. An adult voice sounds different from a child's voice; a violin sounds different from a trumpet

Tone:

i. sound quality produced by a voice or instrument.

ii. the whole space between two adjacent notes/pitches.

Sources of further information

British Kodály Academy – Music Education charity offering advice, resources and courses http://kodaly.org.uk/

Centre for Research in Early Childhood (CREC) – a specialist centre for early childhood research, training and consultancy www.crec.co.uk/

Colourstrings – a Kodály based approach to music education www.colourstrings.co.uk/

Early Childhood Music Education Commission (ECME) – www.isme.org/our-work/commissions-forum/early-childhood-music-education-commission-ecme

European Network of Music Educators and Researchers of Young Children (EuNet MERYC) – a network for people sharing interests about music education and research in relation to young children www.meryc.eu/

MERYC England – early childhood music charitable organisation http://meryc.co.uk/index.html

National Youth Choir of Scotland (NYCoS) – offers support for young people, teachers and choir directors to develop choral singing across Scotland www.nycos.co.uk/

Voices Foundation – a music education charity which aims to help children and young people to learn to sing and develop as musicians www.voices.org.uk/

In the UK you might like to explore your local

➢ Early Years Music Network, such as:

    o North Yorkshire Music Action Zone Early Years Network (NYMAZ)

- o London Early Years Music Network (LEYMN) & Tri-Borough Hub (London)
- o Soundwaves Extra from Take Art (South West England)
- ➢ Library for rhymes and story books

Index

actions *see* movement
adult involvement: parents/carers
   5–8, 11, 27, 58, 62–3; staff,
   other 22, 55
assessment: children 29, 30, 35,
   65–6; curriculum 53, 65; Kolb
   Learning Cycle 68; lessons 58–9,
   78; reflective evaluation 67, 78

babies 5–8, 27–8; attachment 7;
   fabric, use of 82–3; pitch, sense of
   5; pregnancy 5; recorded music
   13; singing with 27–8; songs
   and rhymes, impact of 7, 11,
   17; steady beat 8, 27, 34; vocal
   development 6, 9–10
baby room *see* Young, Vanessa

communication 6, 9, 85
continuous provision: activity
   extension 45, 58, 62; instrument
   provision 94–5

Dionyssiou *see* Infant Directed
   Singing
dynamics 24, 26, 86, 97

environment: home 6, 10, 13;
   physical 55, 57

Forrai, K. 20–1, 33, 65

games 12; group games 19, 23,
   45–8; partner games 19, 44–8;
   solo roles 19, 35; *see also* songs
   and rhymes

Infant Directed Singing 6, 7
Infant Directed Speech 5, 27, 97
inner hearing 13, 23, 24–5, 30, 97
instruments 49, 51, 77–8, 89–90,
   94–5; harmony 50; ostinato 51
interaction: communicative
   musicality 7; social 11; spectrum
   of vocal utterances 7

learning, elements of: anticipation
   47, 48; concentration 12;
   confidence 11–12, 18, 19, 29,
   46, 77, 88; games and rhymes,
   through 19; musical form and
   structure 29, 41–2; imagination
   19, 41, 84; improvisation 30,
   95, 97; kinaesthetic 34; listening
   9, 26, 29, 47, 50, 58; musical
   memory 13, 47; multi-sensory/
   multi modal 12, 18, 98; musical
   styles and genres 20; non-music
   learning 37; notation 19, 98;

sequencing 9, 18, 86; social skills
9, 12, 45–6; speech and language
9, 20, 85; taking turns 25, 29;
team working 19, 45–8, 80;
unconscious learning 17–19, 30,
38, 42, 47
learning objectives 35, 43,
53–4, 58, 71
Lycra: pitch visualisation 25; steady
beat 45–6; team working 19,
45–7; using with objects 45–6,
80–1; see also resources

modelling 18, 20, 22, 43, 50, 72
Moog, H. 10
mother tongue 5, 6, 10, 97
Motherese see Infant Directed Speech
movement (actions) 43, 73–4, 95;
note length, representation of
(duration) 40; pitch, representation
of 25–6; rhythm 39; steady beat
34–5, 44–5, 48; with babies 27
musical concepts: form and structure
19, 29, 41–2, 83, 97; musical
memory 13, 47, 48; relative
concepts 25–6, 86; rests 40–1;
tempo 26, 73; timbre 47, 49, 50,
98; unconscious learning of 13,
17–19, 30, 42

parents 5–8, 11, 27, 58, 62–3
pitch 5, 25–6, 98; accuracy in 13;
children's pitch range 10–11, 21;
men's voices 21; pitch matching
11, 22, 23, 29, 98; puppets 26;
relative pitch 22, 25, 30, 45, 50,
98; represented in movement 25–6
planning 53–65; aims 18,
71–2; continuous provision
62; curriculum 64–5; learning
objectives 35, 43, 53–4, 58, 71;
lessons 53–63, 69–78

practitioners: learning to sing 2;
modelling 18, 20, 22, 43, 50,
72; reflective evaluation 67, 78;
teacher talk 17, 74–5
pulse see steady beat
puppets: to represent dynamics 86;
to represent steady beat 24, 90;
use in games 19; use in singing
22, 23, 24, 26; see also resources

recorded music 13
repetition, importance/effect of
13, 18, 58; babies, with 28;
consistency of 44; singing
development 21; steady beat 35;
variations, adding 75–6
resources 79–96; ball 88–9; bean
bags 41, 93; bells 93; castanet 93;
claves 90; continuous provision,
use in 94–5; fabric, sari 82–3;
fabric (tablecloth) 93; floor spots
93–4; Lycra 45–7, 80–2; magic
22–3, 87–8; parachute 25;
percussion instruments 49–51,
94–5; puppets 19, 22–4, 26, 84–7;
recorder 89–90; scarves 82, 83;
steady beat illustration 24, 90,
94; toys 80, 84; use in games 19;
use in songs 22–4, 26, 76; voice
recorder 95; wooden spoons 91
rests 40, 98; actions during 25, 27,
36, 40–1, 48; floor spots, use
of 93–4
rhythm 33–42, 98; actions
39–40; definition 8, 38; rests
40–1; rhythmic development
33; rhythmic accuracy 11;
rhythmic pattern 39–40; within
songs 39, 71

silent beat see rests
Singese see Infant Directed Singing

singing 9–13, 21–4; as
communication tool 17–18;
children's singing development,
phases 10–11; confidence in
2, 46; cultural heritage 12,
20, 58; emotional security 11;
group singing 12, 23, 41, 44,
73; improvisation 30, 95, 97;
instructions, sung 75; learning
to sing 6; physical experience of
music 12; recorded music 13;
rhythm 37–40; self-confidence
(child) 12; social interaction 11–12;
solo singing 13, 19, 22–3, 29, 88;
stories 45, 47, 58, 62, 63, 76
social and emotional development
11–12; emotional regulation/self-
control 9, 45–6, 47, 80; emotional
security 7–8, 27, 54; see also
learning, elements of
songs and rhymes 17–30, 43–51,
69–71; actions during rests 40–1;
babies 7, 27; call and response
22, 23, 29, 30, 36, 39; choosing
69–70; companion rhyme 46–7;
complexity, developing 18, 19,
46–7, 49–51; complexity of
69–71; dipping rhymes 37, 93;
echo songs 29; form and structure
9, 13, 21, 41–2, 45, 97; game, as
part of 18; instructions, singing 75;
language used in 20; movement
in 18, 33–5, 44–5, 73–4; new
song, introduction of 43, 65; new
songs, number of 65; objects, use
of 76; percussion instruments,
adding 49–50, 77; pitch matching
support 23; pitch visualisation 25;

pot-pourri songs 10, 11; question
and answer 29, 36; repetition,
importance of 13, 18, 21, 28,
47, 75–6; speed/tempo 27, 73;
starting pitch 72; steady beat
73–4; toddlers 28–9; traditional
songs 12, 20, 58; vocabulary
enhancement 9
speech and language 5, 9, 20, 85, 95
steady beat 8, 24, 34–8, 40, 98;
actions 35, 37, 40; floor spots,
use of 93–4; internal sense of
34; movement to 34–5, 44–5,
73–4; puppet's role 24; rhythmic
development 33; see also rests

tempo 26, 98; adjustment of 23, 29;
new song, of 43; speed of song/
rhyme 27, 73
thinking voice see inner hearing
toddlers 28–9
Trehub, S. 7

voice: as instrument 12; care of 56;
child's singing range 21; reading
stories 26; singing solo 22; vocal
development 6, 9–11; voice
control, developing 11, 21, 22,
30; voice pitching 13; voice play
22, 24, 28, 86

Welch, G. 10

Young, S. 66
Young, Vanessa: spectrum of
vocal utterances 7; musical
communication with babies 7–8;
recorded music 13

Printed in Great Britain
by Amazon

78312586R00066